"The end of knowledge is power."

Thomas Hobbes, *Computation, or Logic*, 1665

Definitions in Information Management

A Guide to the Fundamental Semantic Metadata

by

Malcolm D. Chisholm, Ph.D.

Library and Archives Canada Cataloguing in Publication

Chisholm, Malcolm D., 1953-
    Definitions in information management : a guide to the
fundamental semantic metadata / Malcolm D. Chisholm.

Includes bibliographical references and index.

ISBN 978-0-615-35754-6

    1. Information resources management--Dictionaries.
2. Information technology--Management--Dictionaries.

I. Title.

T58.64.C55 2010   658.4'03803   C2010-901720-X

Project Manager – Diane Roblin-Lee, *www.bydesignmedia.ca*
Editor – Denyse O'Leary
Copy Editor – Audrey Dorsch
Indexer – Audrey Dorsch
Interior Design and Layout – Diane Roblin-Lee
Cover Design – Diane Roblin-Lee

Published in Canada by:
byDesign Media
www.bydesignmedia.ca

Printed in the United States of America by:
Lightning Source Inc.

Dr. Chisholm can be contacted via the companion web site for this book:

www.data-definition.com

Acknowledgements

To my family and my teachers

This book is based on my years of experience in data management, during which time I have been privileged to exchange thoughts on the subject with many individuals. I did not keep track of which insights I received from whom, but I know that I have received something from every colleague with whom I have interacted. All I can do therefore is to collectively thank all of these individuals. More recently, I have come across the works listed in the bibliography. While none of these mention data management, their applicability to the discipline will be obvious to any reader. Rather than extend the text with innumerable citations, I will simply state here that nearly all of the ideas in the present work that are not specific to data management have been adapted from these publications

I would like to thank my family for their patience during the preparation of this manuscript.

Table of Contents

One

Introduction to the Use of Definitions in Data Management

ata is the foundation of the Information Age in which we now live. It is the stored representation of facts, and serves not simply as a collective memory of these facts, but also as the basis for sharing information. We have created technology in which data can be manipulated in ways that have immense impact on commerce and society, with the result that it often seems as if technology alone defines the Information Age. Data is more abstract, and perhaps therefore more difficult to appreciate. Yet the significance of data to our modern civilization is enormous even if finding ways to express the importance proves a challenge. It often seems that there is little understanding of what data is and the special problems it presents. Indeed, it is fair to say that data has been mostly taken for granted and rarely thought about in a meaningful way since the beginning of the Information Age in the 1960s. Instead, it is generally supposed that technology – hardware and software – suffices for information management, and that improvements in technology will eventually solve all problems, including those that may arise from data.

When technology is trusted and data is ignored, problems arise. After five decades of the Information Age, there is a risk that these problems may become a crisis. Enterprises across the world have successfully automated business processes and have generated vast quantities of data as a result. Now these same enterprises are trying to integrate the data generated by their applications and develop their applications to keep up with changing environments. And what they are finding is that it is largely impossible. This is a puzzle, because the technology does everything that it is supposed to do, and yet the goals cannot be attained. Gradually, the realization has dawned that significant problems lie in the data itself.

This book is not a survey of the current state of data management. For one thing, it is difficult to get any reliable figures on the degree to which data problems exist. The proposition that large-scale problems exist with data is assumed. Anecdotal examples include the vast amount of money spent on analyzing "as-is" data structures and content in most enterprises. More specifically, the causes of the recent problems in the financial services industry, where data could not be used to properly assess risk, will probably be debated for decades, but they seem to have their roots in the data. It is contended therefore, by many in data management, that we have reached a point where the data in many enterprises is a mess, and it is a mess on many dimensions. This book explores one of these dimensions, possibly the most fundamental one – understanding what data means.

Data always represents something other than itself. It is "about" things. In order for data to be used successfully, it is necessary to completely understand what that data is intended to represent, how it is intended to represent it, and the degree to which it achieves such representation. This is necessary whether it is people or computers that must use the data in question. It may seem an obvious point to make. After all, if we go to the trouble of storing data, surely we must know what it means? Unfortunately, this is not always the case. There is no automatic mechanism that guarantees consistency in the design, population, and interpretation of data involving a host of automated processes and human beings. All too often, data stores are defined in unclear ways, are populated inconsistently, and are misinterpreted when they are used. This may seem like an exaggerated claim, but anyone who disputes it will have to produce evidence to the contrary, and such evidence is sadly lacking in the contemporary literature about data management. In contrast, this literature contains a good deal about topics like "source data analysis," where the objective is to understand existing datasets so they can be used to meet requirements that they were not originally intended to satisfy. "Data quality" problems, about which a good deal has been published, involve issues such as "consistency" where actual data content does not match expected data content. Managing the understanding of what data means – getting to its definition, and getting that definition to wherever it is needed – is therefore a huge task for contemporary data management. But just what is a definition?

What is a Definition?

Perhaps the most natural question a child can ask is "What is it?" Children seem to ask this reflexively, and often with an evident sense of wonder, when they see something for the first time. As we grow older, our experience increases, and both the need to ask the question and our sense of wonder diminish. Once we begin our careers, we realize that if we ever need to ask what something is, we are likely to face a difficult mental exercise that will probably not be a pleasant experience. And yet from time to time in our adult life, we do occasionally ask what something is. We feel more complete for knowing the answer, perhaps recapturing for a fleeting moment the long-forgotten wonder of childhood.

But a child can also ask "What does it mean?," more in puzzle-ment than wonder. The question addresses a spoken or written term, or some other kind of symbol. In asking it, the child wants to share in the experience of human knowledge, to understand how we *represent* the things about which we ask "What is it?" The puzzlement, resulting in the need to ask this question, continues throughout our adult lives. Quite often we encounter unfamiliar terms for concepts we are already aware of. But sometimes we encounter terms that stand for things we have not yet grasped. We come to these new concepts through the terms that represent them – through meaning – rather than by perceiving concrete instances of the concepts themselves. Since data represents things, the need to know what something means is as valid as the need to know what something is when we work with data.

Yet beyond this there are other subtleties in data definitions. Because data is a representation, we need to know how the data represents what it is supposed to represent. Just what is it about something in the "real world" that gets transformed into data? After all, there are practical limits and constraints involved in data. A field that permits a maximum of 80 characters to be stored cannot accommodate a text of 120 characters. Perhaps the text must be abbreviated, or truncated. Such grubby practicalities of data are unavoidable, and we need to understand them too in order to understand the meaning of the data.

The Importance of Data Definitions

We must accept that we need to understand data, but how will we acquire this understanding? Must each person who uses the data independently analyze it and gradually gain the required understanding? Or is there an expectation that data is rather simple stuff, and that the terms that label it convey a sufficient understanding?

A fundamental issue here, which we will return to in more detail, is that in ordinary life we are not constantly in need of definitions. We seem to get along reasonably well with what we have learned by experience. Why should data be any different? The answer seems to be that data really is different because the scale involved is large, and because data deals with things that are not really part of ordinary experience.

In small enterprises the understanding of data may indeed be provided by informal means, such as asking other individuals. But even medium-sized enterprises today have data landscapes with hundreds of thousands of data elements. Common sense tells us that human beings cannot remember what each of these data elements means without somehow committing such definitional knowledge to a permanent record. Furthermore, a significant amount of the data that enterprises manage is not about things that we commonly encounter in everyday life. Enterprises perform very specialized functions, and their data reflects this. Not all of their data perhaps, but enough of it that the whole set cannot be understood from the few cues available. The scale and specialization of enterprise data strongly suggest a need to proactively provide definitions of data for the purpose of management.

Ultimately, all data simply has to be defined because it represents something else. Definitions tell us, or should tell us, what data is intended to mean. Yet, all too often little attention is paid to definitions of data, as if the definition were somehow self–evident. If definitions are important for data, how well are they created and managed today, and how widely are such definitions used? It is very difficult to find reports of assessments of data definitions, and I can really answer only from personal experience.

Having worked in data management in a wide range of enterprises for over 30 years, I have found that there is very little guidance on creating and managing definitions of data. In fact there seems to be an unspoken assumption that data is like words, and data definitions are like dictionary definitions. Yet, I have found that, in practice, data is not like words and requires a much deeper approach than can be provided by definitions modeled after those found in dictionaries. Furthermore, everybody seems to have a personal way of formulating definitions, and where definitions are actually produced they are rarely reviewed in the context of any generally accepted methodology for the structure and content of definitions. Thus, definitions of data, where they exist, are often inadequate to what is required to understand data.

The management of definitions is also, in my experience, poor. Definitions tend to be locked up in specialized tools, such as data modeling software packages, that are not intended to be used widely and feature high-cost licenses that effectively prohibit their general use. Once locked up in these environments, definitions are rarely revisited in any way and remain unimproved. Indeed, it seems to be widely assumed that data definitions are done once and must never change. Definitions can also be also be found scattered throughout various forms of documentation. The same elements are redundantly defined – usually in different ways – in all kinds of artifacts, with varying degrees of quality. This is admittedly part of a more general knowledge management nightmare for most enterprises, but it is particularly true for definitions. It is possible to get some inkling of the scale of the problem. My reviews of completed projects, discussions with other analysts, and information from tool vendors lead me to believe that in any data integration project about 30 percent of the budget is devoted to understanding the data that will be the sources for the project.

Admittedly there is more to source data analysis than understanding data definitions, but definitions are a significant portion. It is as if information technology (IT) is the only area of enterprise that has institutional amnesia. The scale of the waste of resources due to poor knowledge management in IT would horrify executive

management if they truly understood the levels involved.
It is unlikely that executive management will be blind to this
problem forever.

The distribution and usage of data definitions offers a little more
promise. Modern technology is gradually providing more tools
to share knowledge. However, we often find vague underlying
presuppositions that technology alone can solve all the problems
of knowledge management, including data definitions. It cannot.
Furthermore, if software tools are just additional, redundant
containers for poor definitions, they will only add to the scale of
the problem. If the tools are superseded by newer "cool" tools in
a few years, they will quickly fall into disuse. But they will likely
remain as one of the many poorly supported legacy applications
littering IT architectures. There are many difficulties in distrib-
uting definitions and getting stakeholders to use them effectively.
However, the main challenge with data definitions remains forming
and managing them.

What the Experts Say

Given the lack of academic research in this area, expert practi-
tioners in data management were solicited for their views on the
relevance of definitions for information. Here are their comments.

> In today's financial industry, precision and meaning of
> business terms matter. There are literally thousands of data
> attributes, delivered by hundreds of internal and external
> sources – all stored in dozens of unconnected databases.
> That results in lots of mapping, maintenance of cross-
> references, the inconsistent use of terms and way too much
> manual reconciliation. These challenges with precise data
> terms and definitions make it hard to compare data and
> difficult to set precedence rules at an attribute level ... hard
> to automate business processes for better STP ... hard to

exchange data and communication instructions with counterparties ... hard to feed analytical models and calculation engines with confidence ... hard to create consistent benchmarks for meeting the terms of investment agreements ... and hard to do cross-asset risk analysis. – *Michael Atkin, Managing Director, Enterprise Data Management Council*

Definitions offer more to an enterprise than a "Rosetta Stone" of terminology. Given that semantics vary by function within an organization, definitions are rarely universal. But if you *ignore* definitions, you miss out on the opportunity to understand the various business contexts within an enterprise. You miss the opportunity to start the behavior change from "my data" to "our data." Definitions should not be ignored because they are difficult; rather they are a catalyst for progress. – *John Ladley, Founder and President, IMCue Solutions*

Definitions create context and meaning associated with abstract ideas. Without commonality in meaning and context, communication would be difficult, if not impossible. Humans are **implicitly** dependent on proper definitions, whenever we communicate with each other. There needs to be a greater appreciation that definitions must be **explicit** and **precise**, if we are going to get to semantic interoperability between humans and machines. – *Arka Mukherjee, Founder, Global IDs Inc.*

It's easy to understand the importance of definitions when we apply this to our daily life. For example, if someone tells me "I have an interesting job for you," I'm wary. My first question would be "what do you mean by *'interesting?'*" Applying the same wariness when it came to business definitions for data management projects can help avoid common project pitfalls. Including questions such as

"What do you mean by customer (product, employee)?" in requirements planning can help clarify the core business requirements that drive project success. – *Donna Burbank,*
Senior Principal Product Manager,
Computer Associates Erwin Modeling

I find it troubling that in the American educational system, among the other things our children are not taught, in not teaching them how to write, is how to write a definition. This should be basic. But definitions are often vague and misleading.... I have seen very little written on the subject, and I think it is most important. Part of the problem, I suppose, is that everyone assumes that they know how to do it, but they don't. – *David Hay,*
Capgemini Financial Services USA

Pay a little now, or pay a whole lot over time. Definitions should never be an afterthought — they should be front and center to your whole approach. Time and time again we find really big problems boiling down simply to what things really mean. Every report, every query, every transaction, every communication, every requirement, every business rule – *everything* – depends on the business meaning of data. In the big picture, definition management is even more important than data management. Sooner or later, every company will come to understand this ... or not be a player in tomorrow's economy. – *Ron Ross,*
Executive Editor, Business Rules Journal

Getting really good definitions for terms is crucial in almost every aspect of software development and software implementation, but where we find it showing up is at integration time. The incomplete and vague definitions were there all along in the applications being integrated, but somehow the developers and users had finessed their

way around their imprecision with procedures, training, and conventions. But when you try to integrate two systems, it shines a bright light on what is underspecified. Most of the wasted time in systems integration is wasted on late discovery and resolution of bad definitions. Getting precise definitions are an investment in your future.
– *Dave McComb, President, Semantic Arts, Inc.*

What do you mean by _____? After close to 30 years in the consulting business, I think that is the most important single question one can ask during an engagement. What I'm talking about, of course, is the art and science of clarifying communication through good definitions. And it isn't just the end result that matters – the process of building definitions is as important as the destination. Along the way, you find out what *you* really think a term means, what *they* think it means, what that term *might mean* sometime in the future, and any number of other details that will surface and explain miscommunication. I'll never forget the session at which a VP of Marketing leaned out over the table and said to an Accounting Director "You think a Customer is *what?* No wonder those reports you produce are useless to us!" Whether you're working in data management, application requirements, business process management, or business intelligence, everything you produce depends on effective communication, which in turn depends on clear definitions. – *Alec Sharp, Clariteq Inc.*

Effective data definitions are crucial in developing effective systems as well as in communicating effectively. When we just assume that we know what something means, then our systems and communications are prone to huge errors. For example, if we just assume that we know what "customer" means, then this could lead to misunderstandings, operational inefficiencies, and unnecessary time, cost, and effort. For example, does the definition of "customer" include a person or organization that has purchased from us 10 years ago and that is not active? Does it include a prospect that has signed a letter of intent to buy from us? When we produce a "customer report," it would be prudent to have a very clear definition of "customer" in order to avoid confusion, potential liability, additional costs, and miscommunications. – *Len Silverston, Founder and President, Universal Data Models LLC*

Ambiguity is a kind of friction which limits the quality of our discourse, the utility of our data, and the reach of our understanding. All progress in information management depends on our ability to identify its source and reduce it to its absolute minimum. In this regard, no other effort pays more dividends that than of establishing good definitions. – *Suzanne Yoakum-Stover, Ph.D., Executive Director, Institute For Modern Intelligence*

About This Book

From the foregoing statements the reader will appreciate that the central importance of data definitions is hard to deny, and yet it is hard to find much evidence that data definitions concern any enterprise. Given this, it seemed to me that a short inquiry into the theoretical and practical nature of data definitions might be useful, and thus the idea for the current book was born.

The objective of the book is to appreciate definitions in the context of information management. However, the raw material of information is data, so much of the book is specifically targeted to data management. Information is a different topic from data, and there seems to be a permanent debate on just what information is.

It is not practical to enter into that debate here, and this is another reason for a specific focus on data. However, information management, whatever "information" means, is generally accepted to be the goal of information systems. Ultimately, therefore, a good deal of knowledge about the role of definitions in information management will come by aggregating what we come to understand about their role in data management.

This book looks at what definitions are, the different types of definitions, how they are used, how high-quality definitions can be constructed, what problems can exist in definitions, how to manage definitions, and particularly at how to justify work on definitions to executive management. In some ways the area of data definitions is very modern. The proposal of the semantic web is one example. It is based on the idea that if different processes can understand data that is provided to them, then they can use it in a myriad of new ways. Yet, definitions are also a classical problem, stretching, at least in Western thought, as far back as philosophers like Socrates and Aristotle. These early thinkers tried to understand both the things around us and what our knowledge of these things consists of. As we shall see, classical learning has informed modern thought on definitions. Today, however, our problems have multiplied because we are trying to do things with data that have never been attempted before, and on a scale never imagined. It is a challenge that we must face up to, and a large part of that challenge is the successful management of definitions of data.

The intended audience for this book is anyone involved in building, managing, and using data assets. This will, of course, include data analysts and business analysts, but it also extends to IT managers, developers, and business users who make decisions based on data content. Although the book focuses primarily on data, it is hoped that it might be useful in other areas – particularly the analysis and design of business processes, and the management of IT infrastructure. To this end a brief glossary of technical data management terms is provided in *Appendix 1*.

The topic of data definition is connected with many other problems of information management, and it has sometimes been difficult to decide where one ends and the other begins. These borderlands are frequently encountered in the book. In such gray areas the approach of keeping strictly to definitions has been chosen, rather than exploring the regions that lie beyond it. Hopefully this has given the book a length and focus that will prove satisfactory to the reader.

Finally, there is a companion website for the book:

http://www.data-definition.com

This website will provide additional material on definitions in information management that readers may find of interest.

Two

Justifying Definitions in Data Management

It may seem odd to begin an examination of definitions with ways in which they can be justified. However, it is the logical place to start. In the first place, people who might be interested in definition management will be looking for reasons why they should really care. Unless some reasons can be given why they should, they will be justified in moving on to other areas that at least make specific promises about how data management can be improved. More important, definition management is a relatively new area, and if it is to be implemented in any enterprise, resources must be allocated to it. Only executive management can do this, and they must be given a compelling value proposition for why they should allocate any such resources. Therefore, it is from the perspective of executive management that we look here at the roles that definitions play in data management in order to justify the good management of data definitions.

It is common to think of executive managers as merely powerful, but they face enormous pressures and have relatively little time in which to make decisions about new initiatives. Explaining to them the abstract theory of definitions is not a way to get their attention. They must first be told why definition management is worthwhile. Then, if they are interested, they will want to hear more about what definitions are. Justification must precede explanation.

Definitions of data have been long thought to be important in data management, although that should not be taken to mean that they have often been successfully addressed. Nor is the mere idea that they are important a justification for an enterprise devoting any resources to dealing with definitions.

A recurrent danger in data management is to think that things are "good" by their very nature, and not to spend much time identifying precisely why they are good. This is seldom accompanied by much thought about how to implement such things. Definitions present this danger, because it seems rather silly to argue that they are not "good," and it initially appears relatively uncomplicated to "do definitions." However, executive management will be unwilling to allocate resources to any activity for which no detailed explanation can be produced either for its immediate benefits or its implementation. Furthermore, exercises that executive management perceive as "academic" are less likely to be funded. We need, therefore, to consider precisely what definitions can be used for, and then to show how these uses can offer practical value to the average enterprise.

Let us therefore try to justify definitions by looking at the roles they play in data management. For the moment we will not worry about the nature of definitions and what makes them special in data management. These topics will be examined in more detail in later chapters.

General Requirements for Definitions

We will first consider general roles definitions play in data management, and then examine some specific data management tasks where definitions can be helpful.

1. Use of Definitions to Understand Business Concepts Represented in Data

A definition provides an understanding of a concept. Data represents things, and all things are instances of concepts. With clear definitions of concepts, data becomes more understandable and thus more usable. High-quality definitions will help everyone know the business of the enterprise better. The better a definition, the better everyone can use the data it applies to.

All enterprises have a number of strange terms signifying specialized concepts. We tend to call these terms "jargon," which really refers more to the strange *names* by which these concepts are called. An enterprise that wants to hire a new employee tends to prefer someone who "knows the business," because that person will likely already be familiar with the jargon and what it means. However, it is often not possible to get new hires with such experience.

Staff who are recent joiners, and thus not yet fully acquainted with the enterprise's jargon, will better understand the information systems of the enterprise if data definitions are available. Yet even staff who have been with the business for a while may be unsure about information outside their particular local specialty, so definitions can be useful to them too. This is especially true for IT staff, who tend to know a good deal about IT but much less about the business, yet must nevertheless manage the information resource of the enterprise. The extent to which lack of definition management impacts IT staff does not seem easy to ascertain. Anecdotal evidence may be the best we have. For instance, during the early years of my career in IT, I made many mistakes and wasted a lot of time due to misunderstanding items of data. On reflection, I realized that in such cases I always came away thinking "If only I had known what that really meant."

Failure to understand what concepts mean must have an impact on enterprises even beyond IT, but the extent is difficult to estimate. Nevertheless, as enterprises increasingly embrace a culture of knowledge, and our economy becomes more oriented to information, logic dictates that definitions will be necessary and must be managed.

2. Use of Definitions to Disambiguate Terms

Terms are really nothing more than arbitrary labels for concepts. Unfortunately, the technical jargon in all enterprises can make it quite difficult to precisely indentify the concepts they signify, let alone help in understanding these concepts. For instance, a user may encounter a situation where he or she thinks that two terms apply to the same concept. But is this really the case, or do the two terms apply to different concepts?

The only way to solve this problem in the long run for all users in an enterprise is to have access to clear definitions that disambiguate the terms. Users can then know whether a term used to signify an item of data is unique, a synonym, or a homonym.

Yet the problem can become even more complex than this. There can be subtle differences within an enterprise, so that two terms may be synonymous in one context, but not in another. In the Marketing Department "customer" and "client" may be synonyms for the same concept, but Marketing's definition of "customer" may not match Finance's definition of "client." We will explore this problem in detail later, but for now it is important to appreciate that the only way to quickly overcome such a problem is to have appropriate definitions available that can quickly and easily be consulted, and confidently used.

3. Understanding Metadata Versus Data

One of the fundamental characteristics of data is that, while it represents something else, it is actually a distinct thing in its own right. Aspects of data that apply to data itself are often termed "metadata." When we look at a data object like a record in a database table, it is important to know which parts of it are metadata and which are not. This duality – the data itself and what it represents – is a problem that makes data difficult to deal with. For instance, we may have a record with a column called *Update Date*. Is that an attribute of the thing the data is representing, or is it metadata that belongs to the record itself, in which case it has nothing to do with what the record represents?

Definitions can help us separate what the data represents from metadata, which describes the data itself. The metadata may be interesting for some purposes, but a business user is unlikely to be concerned about it when working with purely business data. The same can also be true for a data analyst. For example, when comparing what is thought to be the same data in two different applications, the analyst will probably initially want to focus only on what the data represents – the underlying business concepts. The metadata is likely to be confusing and should be excluded until a later stage.

4. Identification of an Instance to a Concept

A basic function of definitions is to answer the question "What kind of thing is that?" where we have a vague idea of what an individual thing might be. This is similar to the challenge faced every day by physicians when they try to diagnose diseases. Data entry operators, in particular, may sometimes need to input information that is rather different from what they are used to seeing. The need to assign an instance (an individual thing) to a concept (a type of thing) is often encountered when trying to select an option from a drop-down list during data entry. To make this problem clearer, let us consider an example.

Suppose a data entry operator must enter information about companies and the industrial sector they operate in. In this instance, the operator must enter information for a company that provides consulting services in philosophy. The application uses the North American Industry Classification System (NAICS), the standard used by the US government for classifying business establishments.

NAICS is very widely used and is a comprehensive standard. Unfortunately, it has no entry for philosophy as an economic activity. There is a sector 54 entitled "Professional Scientific and Technical Services," defined as follows:

> The Professional, Scientific, and Technical Services sector comprises establishments that specialize in performing professional, scientific, and technical activities for others. These activities require a high degree of expertise and training. The establishments in this sector specialize according to expertise and provide these services to clients in a variety of industries and, in some cases, to households. Activities performed include: legal advice and representation; accounting, bookkeeping, and payroll services; architectural, engineering, and specialized design services; computer services; consulting services; research services; advertising services; photographic services; translation and interpretation services; veterinary services; and other professional, scientific, and technical services.

> This sector excludes establishments primarily engaged in providing a range of day-to-day office administrative services, such as financial planning, billing and recordkeeping, personnel, and physical distribution and logistics. These establishments are classified in Sector 56, Administrative and Support and Waste Management and Remediation Services.

This seems closer to philosophy than any other sector, and certainly does not seem to exclude philosophy. However, there is more detail available in NAICS, and one is generally required to choose an industry within a sector. Looking under sector 54, there is no philosophy industry, but there is an industry that might reasonably contain it: 541720 – "Research and Development in the Social Sciences and Humanities." This is defined as

> This industry comprises establishments primarily engaged in conducting research and analyses in cognitive development, sociology, psychology, language, behavior, economic, and other social science and humanities research.

> Cross-References. Establishments primarily engaged in marketing research are classified in Industry 541910, Marketing Research and Public Opinion Polling.

Again, even if the company in question is not a research company but directly provides philosophy services, this entry seems to match most closely.

We would expect the data entry operator to search though the NAICS definitions in this way and assign the closest matching NAICS code to the philosophy consulting company. Difficult as this may be, it would be certainly a lot more difficult and error-prone without the NAICS definitions.

This example is important because data is entered into many applications at all times in all enterprises, and is at the initial point of data entry where many data quality problems are created. Once a mistake has been made in data it can be very difficult to correct. Stopping data quality problems at the point of origin is generally accepted as the best way of dealing with them. Definitions are one of the few supporting tools that can achieve this.

Yet issues of identification can be found in other areas as well. It is particularly important in accounting. There can be considerable difficulty in "booking" an item of income or expenditure. It is necessary to "recognize" the flow of money involved and place it appropriately in an electronic journal. Very often, specific fields must be updated for certain accounting entries. For instance, a credit card issuer will need to know for each type of card issued precisely what "Finance Charges" actually means. Might it include Overlimit Fees and Annual Membership Fees?

Definitions thus help us to identify the concept to which an instance belongs. Without definitions a lot more guesswork and poorer data quality are inevitable.

5. Consistency of Derivation or Computation

Some fields in databases have values that are derived or computed from other fields. In these cases, we expect program logic to execute the actual derivation or computation, unlike, say, a field whose values are data-entered on a screen by a human operator.

If we have a precise definition of the computation or derivation, then it is possible to determine if the value in the field is correct or not. This kind of auditing can be very useful, but it requires a precise definition.

If no such definition is present, or it is not trusted, there is only one alternative. This is to reverse engineer the program logic that performs the derivation or computation. That may not be an easy task. Many applications are vendor-supplied "black boxes" where the program source is protected intellectual property that is not available for examination and thus cannot be reverse engineered. Other applications are "legacy" applications, where the source may be written in an outdated programming language that is difficult or impossible for current staff to understand. Even applications that are understandable may be so complex that they cannot easily be reverse engineered. A good definition that states the algorithm of the computation or derivation can be extremely useful in these circumstances.

If a derived or computed field must be reverse engineered, the results obtained should be kept in a definition. In this way the reverse engineering need be done only once. If the results are not retained, then the reverse engineering may have to be repeated, which would be an unjustifiable waste of resources.

6. Use of Definitions to Compare Concepts in Data Mapping

Quite often in dealing with data, terms are not relevant. We are simply presented with two sets of data and we need to know if the data represents the same things or different things. The terms involved, such as the table and column names, are at best clues to meaning, but cannot be relied upon. A significant part of determining if two sets of data describe the same things is to understand the concepts that the data represents. The only way to do this is to arrive at definitions. When we obtain the definitions for what two different data sets are supposed to represent, we can compare them and determine if they truly overlap or differ. Of course, to function this way, the definitions must be of good quality. If they are not of good quality, we may be confused or misled.

These kinds of exercises are often called "data mapping." If one set of data "maps" to another set, then they are identical. The specialized concepts in most enterprises inevitably make data mapping exercises difficult. However, the need to integrate data has grown rapidly in recent years, and many enterprises confront the need to carefully compare the concepts associated with different data sets. Yet they often lack sufficiently detailed definitions.

Data mapping may also be required when data lineages are traced. For instance, a business user may question some data on a report. An analyst may then need to trace that data to its source. Very often, reports are not built on the database on which the data is first produced but on a database where the data is copied from some other database. There may be a chain of databases, with data copied from one to the next. As the analyst works out the pathway by which the data arrived in the report, he or she must ensure that the data is the same as it moves from one database to another. Definitions can be used to assess the data at each stage, to ensure it is not undergoing changes.

The value of definition in data mapping is also necessary for what is called the "semantic web" and similar projects. The semantic web is a relatively new idea in information processing: if computers could understand what data meant, then they could process it with far less intervention by human beings and could process disparate data content shared over the Internet. Clearly, definitions are necessary for this. Whether the faith placed in such projects is well founded is, however, another matter.

7. Comparison of Data Content to Definition Within a Single Field

It is easy to see how a definition may be useful for a derived or computed field, but definitions are also relevant to fields that are populated via data entry or updated with information taken from other fields. In these cases it is possible to some extent to determine if the data content of the data object matches its supposed definition. In other words, does the data *actually* mean what it is *supposed* to mean? For instance, if we see that the field Date of Birth contains what is obviously a telephone number, we immediately know it represents something other than what its name suggests, and there is probably a data quality issue.

Fields in databases or other data stores can drift away from their original storage intent. Without a high-quality definition, a field may degenerate into a storage area for all kinds of different data. Creating or enabling this kind of disorder is a failure of data governance. This may be controllable within a single application where the program logic can be adjusted to accommodate the changing types of data stored in the field. However, such data will not be sharable outside the application where the data is maintained without replicating the complex program logic that has grown up to manage it.

Good definitions can permit periodic exercises where the data content is compared to the data definitions, and the determination made if the data is drifting away from its original intent. Ideally, this drift can be stopped or reversed.

Such pressure on data is to be expected. Enterprises must continually change to meet new challenges. Databases rarely change in step with the business side of the enterprise, partly because operationalization of change is not thorough enough to reach the databases. When sudden, unexpected demands are placed on databases, the response may be to reuse existing fields for new purposes. There are no obvious easy answers to these problems, but good definitions can at least identify them clearly.

Figure 2.1 summarizes the general roles played by definitions in data management. These could be used as a point of departure for the formulation of more detailed use cases.

(See Fig. 2.1, p. 34.)

Justification in Business Context

The above list shows how definitions may be important in a number of activities. Even if executive managers understand and agree with the list, they may still question whether these activities warrant the allocation of resources to the specific promotion of high-quality definitions. They will probably note that most enterprises have got along without definition management for a long time. Why spend money on it now? There are several answers.

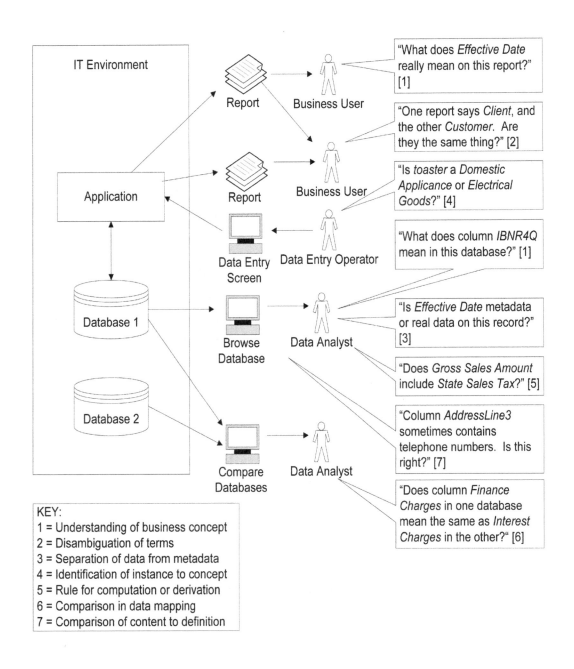

Figure 2.1: *Summary of General Roles for Definitions in Data Management*

1. Source Data Analysis (SDA)

For several decades, applications were built to automate business processes. Today, most of those processes have been automated. As a result, demand has switched to information applications, where the data produced in the transaction applications is copied to other environments where it is integrated and enriched so that it can be analyzed to meet a variety of needs such as monitoring competitive position, determining efficiency of processes, and so on. This domain of information management is usually termed "business intelligence" (BI).

Systems analysts and business analysts who formerly participated in the implementation of new transaction applications are now much more likely to work on BI projects. A good part of their effort consists of source data analysis (SDA), that is, understanding the data in source databases that must be moved over and integrated into the BI environment. This is quite different from the work done in years past of automating business processes. That involved understanding data within the context of a single business process that typically involved a single user group that would directly benefit from the automation of the process involved. BI typically involves multiple databases with the involvement of user groups who will not all equally be the beneficiaries of the new environment, and some of whom are less inclined to be of assistance. In any case, each user group understands only their environment and is not well positioned to compare this data with the data in the other environments than other user groups.

Thus, SDA is fundamentally different from "analysis" in the context of building new transaction applications. This also helps to explain why definitions are much more important today than they were in the past. The old methodologies used to build applications were essentially focused on custom software development. They have much less relevance to BI projects, where data that already exists is being combined to provide value to areas other than those that produced it. The emphasis in SDA is clearly on understanding the existing data, and there can be little argument that definitions are necessary.

2. Analysis Rework

In theory, if all data objects were defined fully, and the definitions adhered to by developers and users, SDA would not be necessary. This is true not only for building BI applications, but also for a variety of other tasks. For instance, if a transaction application is to be replaced by another, a "gap analysis" of the data will need to be done. Does the data in the existing application match the data in the proposed new one? Another example might be production data support, where errors and exceptions must be analyzed to understand what has gone wrong. This typically requires understanding the data.

A common theme in all of this is that information technology (IT) is not good at remembering what it has already done, especially in regard to data. As a result, analysis tasks that involve data must often be repeated. A large proportion of the analysts employed by enterprises are now essentially examining what IT has already done and are trying to understand it. Worse yet, the same data is examined over and over again, often to answer the same questions asked at different times.

If analysts created and stored high-quality definitions for data objects, then their work would provide an input to any further data analysis on the same data objects. Today, in SDA the focus tends to be on getting an understanding that is "good enough" for the immediate task at hand – an understanding that is frequently of no greater duration than a project. Any information gathered tends to be documented in a way that hinders understanding outside of the immediate task or project, and indeed little thought is given to the prospect that the information gathered might be used in any future work.

Definition management can go a long way to reducing unnecessary analysis rework. It can also significantly shorten the time taken to perform analysis tasks.

3. Data Integration

Formerly, most IT environments consisted of stand-alone applications that did not exchange data with each other. These are commonly known as "silos." Today, almost every enterprise recognizes that data is a useful resource. However, in order to get value out of data, one must take it from its silos and integrate it. Although this would seem like a simple technical endeavor, it is not.

Many silos have existed for years, and typically provide functionality for a well-defined group within the enterprise. The individuals that work in this group have become familiar with the quirks of their silo – of which there are always far more than is generally recognized. In order to deal with system oddities, these individuals often adopt strange terminology and adapt common terms to mean something unusual in the context of the silo.

When data integration is attempted, it is assumed that the data taken from silos is easily understood. Perhaps a good deal of it may be, but there are nearly always a lot of issues. For instance, a legacy application might be able to define only accounts and not customers, but may be used in such a way that a special account format represents a customer. This will be difficult to appreciate at the beginning of a data integration exercise.

The only reliable way to determine if data can be integrated is by semantic analysis, i.e., understanding the meaning of the data. In other words, we need definitions. Much of this work is SDA, as discussed above. However, it is worth emphasizing that data integration is a distinct area because executive management is typically highly concerned about it. The most extreme forms of integration projects occur during mergers and acquisitions, where the overall data environments of two organizations must be combined.

Yet integration requires more than SDA can provide. Integration processes create new data from multiple existing sources. The procedure must be carefully documented so that the data in the new environments is fully understood. The whole will not be a sum of the parts. That is, the target data in the integrated environment cannot be expected to be the sum of the data in the sources, nor will it be one source selected over others. Thus existing definitions may not always be reusable, and new ones will be required. These new definitions will be far more complex because the integrated data has been manipulated to a greater extent than the source data, which lies closer to the point of data entry and thus to the pure business concepts. The challenge in integration is *not* to add to the data mess seen in most enterprises. Unsustainable complexity that initially works is easy to create, but an integration environment that is simple and more sustainable over the long term is a much more difficult challenge.

Overcoming Objections

We have examined the role of definitions in data management primarily as a way of justifying the need for definition management, and thereby seeing how it can be applied. However, it is worth remembering that it is the job of senior management to ask tough questions and it is worth anticipating what such questions may be.

No senior executive is likely to ask why definitions should be managed now when they were never needed in the past, as they risk some deliciously sarcastic responses. But there is still some merit to this question. Why did data management only now become a pressing issue? The answer is that we were all focused on building applications in the past, and not on managing data. Data management was oriented in past years to a different set of requirements from those that exist today. Data management must accept some share of responsibility for the data mess in most enterprises, but now is the time to address the problem.

Another question that may be raised is, if activities such as data modeling did address definition management in the past, what has changed today? Perhaps all we have to do is be more diligent in what we were always doing. The answer is that very little guidance on data definitions was provided in the past, and, frankly, the role of definitions was not understood. Today, we understand that a better approach to definition management is required if we are to solve the difficult problems of data management.

Yet another question is whether simply adopting technology is all that is required. This is more of an attitude than a question. IT staff have always built things better than they have managed them, and are most comfortable when a piece of technology can be put in place that will solve a problem. The IT staff can then move on to other things, with only the need to ensure that the piece of infra-structure continues to function. Such an attitude will not suffice for definitions. No piece of technology will solve this problem, which requires long-term management. This attitude is one reason for thinking that, in the long run, data management must be divorced from IT, but that is an entirely different topic. For the moment, data management personnel can only be aware of the shortcomings of the current approach and try everything possible to show the need for a different way of doing things.

No doubt, other objections to definition management will be encountered, some of which will be specific to particular enter-prises. Data management staff must clearly understand the roles that definitions play, and must develop concrete plans to imple-ment them.

Definitions Versus Images

Three

We have now seen that definitions are needed for data management. And yet, it often seems that definitions are not of primary concern in data management. Drawing data models, and specifying relationships among their entity types, has always been a good deal more popular than formulating the definitions for their components. This may be due in part to confusion about whether definitions can be substituted by other logical constructs that serve just as well, if not better. The obvious candidate for this role is images, as the popularity of data model diagrams seems to witness.

We live in a visual age and are constantly bombarded with images delivered through a variety of media channels. Both the channels and the number of images seem to be multiplying. The effect on our culture is hard to discern, but there seems to be an increased appetite for "visual learning" as time pressures permit less and less attention to the printed word. It is almost astonishing to think that only 100 years ago books were not only the principal medium of instruction but also the principal form of entertainment.

The question naturally arises, therefore, as to how images and definitions differ. After all, if we need only a visual representation such as a data model diagram, then perhaps the complexity of definitions is unnecessary. It also seems a lot easier to deal with mental images than with definitions.

Mental Images

When we imagine something, we form a mental picture of it. The ancient Greeks termed this a *phantasm*. I can readily form mental pictures of all kinds of things. The more familiar I am with them, the more detailed the phantasm will be. For instance, I can easily form mental pictures of members of my family, my house, my car, and so on. On the other hand, it is more difficult to form a clear mental picture of things I with which I have only a limited acquaintance. For instance, I have never eaten a white truffle and am not sure what one looks like.

Conception is a different matter. When I form a concept of something, I have a much deeper understanding than I can get with the power of imagination. For instance, I can use my intellect to separate out the different attributes of the thing conceived. I consider these attributes carefully and define them. I place them in hierarchies, and find out which are unique to the object I am considering and which are shared with other objects. I try to place the object in groups that I already know about. Additionally, I tease out the rules by which this thing behaves, to understand how its attributes change their determinations, perhaps independently, perhaps in coordination with others, and perhaps in response to events external to the thing conceived.

We all do this, and thus we understand how the thing conceived is possible in its own right. If we put all these ideas together, we can form a good definition. At this point, we are still talking about things around us, rather than data, but we can begin to understand the difference between an image and a definition.

Example of Image Versus Definition

Let us try a simple thought experiment to contrast images with definitions. Try to imagine a talking stone. I am doing it now. In my mind I can see it. It is rounded, although not as thick as it is wide. In color, it is various shades of gray with a couple of white streaks of something like calcite running through it. On one edge there is a mouth with thin lips and a good set of white teeth. The stone has a tongue and is speaking to me in English. It is telling me that the weather is a little colder than yesterday, and that there might be rain this afternoon.

Now I am going to try to imagine a mortgage-backed security (MBS). I cannot. In my mind I see the curbside vendors outside the New York Stock Exchange who sell antique bond certificates. But the characteristics of an MBS have nothing to do with paper and its decorative printing. In any case, I am fairly sure that MBSs came after all bonds were dematerialized and no longer printed as certificates. I try again. This time I see a sorry chain of events beginning with a crafty mortgage broker in Irvine, California, and ending with a gullible bank depositor in Oslo, Norway. But this does not help me visualize an MBS either – it is much more about actors in a set of processes than a static thing called an MBS. Now I try to think of how an MBS fits with all the things related to it, such as trusts, trustees, special purpose vehicles, deals, series, tranches, credit enhancements, rating agencies, event triggers, and so on. Yet I cannot form a mental image of any of these either, so they are of no help in imagining an MBS.

Nobody can form a mental picture of a mortgage-backed security.

However, even though I cannot imagine an MBS I can certainly form a detailed concept of it. I can do this because I have been involved with so many securitization-related computer systems that I am very well aware of the concept of an MBS, of its attributes, behavior, relationships, and management needs. For instance, I know that servicing can be sold separately from the underlying debt obligation, giving the impression to mortgage holders that the company they pay every month is actually their "lender," whatever a lender might be in the case of an MBS. A large part – if not all – of this conceptualization could be considered the definition of an MBS.

Thus, there are major differences between a talking stone and a mortgage-backed security, at least as regards image and definition. I can easily imagine the talking stone, even if such a thing could not possibly exist. But I will never be able to form an image in my mind of an MBS, a thing which certainly does exist. I cannot form a coherent concept of a talking stone that is not filled with ambiguities and impossibilities. Yet I can describe the nature and characteristics of an MBS in enough detail that a listener would end up with a sound understanding of this class of financial instrument. More important, I can do this in conjunction with many others so that we can collaboratively build computer applications to manage MBSs.

The Scale of the Problem

It might be argued that a mortgage-backed security is rather unusual and exotic. Perhaps so, but it is equally difficult to form mental images of things like insurance policies, sales, bank accounts, overdrafts, fees, and a myriad of other financial entities that are the heart of many enterprise information systems. Even where we might think we can form reasonable mental images, we may not really be doing so. How can the image of a customer differ from that of a person? How can an image of a product type differ from that of an assemblage of different manufactured things?

Without these distinctions we are not really visualizing a customer or product type, but something else that is easier, more concrete, and more familiar. And in any case, each person who forms such images is likely to form quite different images from others. The lack of precision and the wide divergence in these images make them of little use as substitutes for definitions. They cannot even be communicated easily.

The Information Age requires a good deal more conceptualization than imagination. Mental images lack the precision needed to build systems to manipulate information. This is because mental images are mere pictures that do not separate out and define the attributes, behavior, and relationships of the object imagined. Unfortunately, conceptualization is very difficult, as anyone involved in building computer applications can testify. It is as if we are working in a twilight world where we are aware of things but cannot "see" them clearly.

Precise definitions give us a major piece of the conceptualization we need for each object that is to be represented in an information system. A reliance on images may be acceptable in other areas of human endeavor, but that simply will not do for data. It is important to understand this distinction because it is not always brought out, and it remains as a nagging doubt about definitions in the minds of many people. If they are used to images and visual learning, they may find dealing with definitions as somehow unnatural because it is unfamiliar. Data and business analysts who engage in definition management should be aware of these attitudes, and they need to think carefully about how definition management should be implemented and what supportive training may be required.

Four

Theory and History of Definities

T he need for definitions in data management is a relatively recent development, but definitions have a considerable history in Western thought and have been considered very important for millennia. Today, most people in the West tend to view definitions as applying to words and expect them to be found in dictionaries. However, in the past, definitions were seen as fundamental to philosophy and logic, and not merely as one topic among others in lexicography. Understanding the varied ways in which past generations treated definitions can help us to better appreciate what can and cannot be expected of them today.

Before we can examine the history of definitions, it is first necessary to understand something of the theory on which definitions rest. Of course, this theory was built up over the centuries and is itself a product of historical processes, particularly in logic. Nevertheless, the theory presents a fairly coherent framework within which the unique properties of definitions can be understood. This framework contains a number of important components, and we will first review them and then see how they are used in definitions.

The Sign

A sign is something that represents something else.

Signs can be material, like traffic signs, in which case a physical object is visible. We see a traffic sign and then understand that it is "telling us something," such as to stop or yield. However, material signs have little relevance in information management, where we are wholly concerned about formal signs. A formal sign is nothing more than a sign. A material sign always has something more to it, like the pole, plate, and metal content of a stop sign.

It should be noted that today there is a growing need to manage things like flags, badges, insignia, logos, and the like as part of data. Traditionally these signs have been important in just a few areas, such as military affairs and sports. As the volume of video, image, and signal data increases, the need to identify and interpret signs in such data presents a considerable data management challenge. Traditionally, the scientific and intelligence communities have focused on this problem, but awareness seems to be increasing in mainstream data management.

However, despite their increasing importance, these kinds of signs are still a tiny fraction of the data processed in nearly all enterprises. What is most important for data management is one subclass of signs – terms.

The Term

A term is a written or verbal expression that simply, by convention among a group of people, is a sign that stands for a concept.

Sometimes the word "name" may be used for the word "term." For instance, the English philosopher Thomas Hobbes wrote:

> A Name is a word taken at pleasure to serve as a mark which may raise in our mind a thought like to some thought we had before, and which being pronounced to others, may be to them a sign of what thought the speaker had before in his mind. *[Computation or Logic, 1655].*

So traditional logic tells us that a term is a word or group of words that is nothing more than a label to signify a concept. There are a few problems with this for data management.

- A term (a group of words) may refer to an instance and not a concept. For example, "Socrates" or "Julius Caesar" refer to instances (of people), whereas "Philosopher" and "Emperor" refer to concepts (types of people, in this case). While terms can signify instances as well as concepts, definitions (as we shall see) can apply only to concepts and not to instances. Therefore, a term will not always signify a concept.

- The nature of the convention needed for general agreement on what is signified by a term is quite arbitrary. It can change over time. For example, the term "sophisticated" means clever and fashionable today, but in the past it was an insult suggesting the unscrupulous methods of the ancient Sophists, who would "prove" any point they were paid to prove. In many enterprises, changes in culture, especially where mergers and acquisitions occur, can lead to such shifts in convention. Terms will then signify concepts that are different from those they signified before.

- Convention only applies among a group of people. Large enterprises often tend to be groupings of rather self-contained communities. Hence the Marketing department may use a given term, like "customer," in a different way from the Accounts Receivable department. Failure to understand this can cause considerable problems in definition management.

We will return to these problems with terms in later chapters.

The Concept

The concept is perhaps the most important idea related to data definition because it is concepts that have definitions. However, it is very difficult to get an adequate definition of a concept. Table 4.1 shows some examples:

Table 4.1: *Definitions of "Concept"*

	Source	Definition of Concept
1	Wordnet (http://wordnetweb. princeton.edu)	**concept**, conception, construct (an abstract or general idea inferred or derived from specific instances)
2	*Baldwin's Dictionary of Philosophy and Psychology* (1) Definition of "conception" with "concept" (2) Definition of "conception" with "universal"	(1) Cognition of a universal as distinguished from the particulars which it unifies. The universal apprehended in this way is called a Concept. (2) The term Universal stands for any mode in which particular experiences are unified so as to form a single whole which is identified as the same throughout the variety of its parts, phases, or aspects... ...There is one point in our definition of conception which requires to be specially emphasized. Conception is the 'cognition

Source	Definition of Concept
(Cont'd)	of a universal as distinguished from the particulars which it unifies.' The words 'as distinguished from' are of essential importance. The mere presence of a universal element in cognition does not constitute a concept. Otherwise all cognition would be conceptual. The simplest perception includes a universal. In perceiving the colour red I recognize it as the same in various moments of its appearance. In order to conceive red, I must do more than this; I must draw a distinction between its general nature and its particular appearances. The universal must be apprehended in antithesis to the particulars which it unifies. This is a process which probably cannot take place except in a very rudimentary form without the aid of language.
3	Merriam–Webster's Online Dictionary (http://www.merriam webster.com/diction-ary/data)	• Function: *noun* • Etymology: Latin *conceptum*, neuter of *conceptus*, past participle of concipere to conceive – more at conceive • Date: 1556 1: something conceived in the mind : thought, notion 2: an abstract or generic idea generalized from particular instances

(Table 4.1 continued on page 52.)

	Source	Definition of Concept
4	Cambridge Advanced Learner's Dictionary online (http://diction-ary.cambridge.org/define.asp?key=19660 &diet=CALD)	concept Show phonetics noun [C] a principle or idea: *The very concept of free speech is unknown to them.* *It is very difficult to define the concept of beauty.* *I failed to grasp the film's central concept.* *Kleenbrite is a whole **new** concept **in** toothpaste!*

Table 4.1: *Definitions of "Concept"*

A concept has been called a "universal nature." It is the answer to the question "What is that?" Our minds understand that there are *kinds* of things that exist in the universe, and we grasp that every individual thing that exists is an example of a kind of thing, and a kind of thing is a concept. Yet, the concept itself exists only in our minds, and is not a physical thing.

In data management, the concept usually corresponds to the entity (more properly called "entity type") found in data models. Data models are the diagrammatic (usually) representations of database designs. However, data modelers can design entity types that do not correspond to concepts, and they do so far more frequently than is realized. Ideally, entity types are implemented as tables in physical databases, and thus tables correspond to concepts. As we shall see later, tables may actually end up corresponding to mixtures of concepts.

Entity types and tables are not the only data objects that can correspond to concepts. Sometimes, individual records in a database table can represent concepts. We saw in Chapter 2 the example of the North American Industrial Classification System (NAICS). This can be implemented as a table in which every record represents an industry. Thus one record may exist for NAICS Code "711212." This number stands for "Racetracks" and is defined as follows:

> This U.S. industry comprises establishments primarily engaged in operating racetracks. These establishments may also present and /or promote the events, such as auto, dog, and horse races, held in these facilities.

Thus "Racetrack" is a concept in NAICS and will be represented by a single record in an NAICS database table. The NAICS table represents the more general concept of the NAICS classification itself.

Concepts go a long way toward making knowledge possible. Because they describe a universal nature, the individual things that fall within a concept have a commonality that we almost take for granted. We know what a rose is because we understand the concept of the rose. If we are told a certain thing is a rose, then we will expect it to possess certain attributes, such as rose-shaped petals, and we will be aware that we may need to handle it carefully because it may have thorns.

In relational databases the same holds true. We can represent something like a bank account as a table, the columns of which represent attributes that we expect every bank account to have. Once we have implemented the table, we can store information about actual bank accounts as records in it, and each one will reflect the universal nature of the concept of the bank account.

While all this may seem like just so much common sense, there have been challenges to the idea of the concept over the centuries.

- **Nominalism** is a philosophy that denies the concept and holds that there are no common natures shared by individual things. If this were true, we could not construct relational database tables to hold information about individual things because each such thing would be utterly unique. Obviously, this is not the case, so nominalism is not a practical idea for data management.
- **Conceptualism** is a different philosophy, which holds that concepts exist but apply to all individual things. In practical terms, this is pretty much the same as nominalism. Again, it is difficult to see how this approach could be helpful in any way to data management. The notion that we must create a separate database table for every individual bank account seems impractical and unrewarding.

The Instance

Concepts are ideas that we hold in our minds about the commonality that exists among individual things in the universe. If we accept the idea of concepts as outlined above, we will find that every individual thing that we come across in the universe can be assigned to one or more concepts. This is perhaps a rather mysterious state of affairs, but a happy one for data management because it greatly helps us in designing data stores.

The individual things in the universe are *instances* of individual concepts. I can say of myself than I am an instance of a human being, and also an instance of a mammal, and also an instance of a vertebrate.

An instance is therefore an individual thing that implements a concept.

The word "instance" can be a little tricky to deal with in data management, because it is often used to refer to a record in a relational database table. In actual fact, a record is a representation of an instance. John Doe will have a record for himself in the patient database in his doctor's office. That record represents the instance of a human being (John Doe), but it is just a record and not actually John Doe.

Unfortunately, for shorthand in data management, we tend to speak of such a record as if it were actually John Doe. A doctor may say to his assistant, "Bring up John Doe on the computer." This would probably be fine, except that an individual record is also an instance of something else – the concept of the record. Keeping straight in our minds the instance that is being represented in the record, and the need to manage the record as a record, irrespective of what it represents, is not easy. These mental gymnastics are what makes data management so difficult, but also so interesting.

With this caution, let us consider one further feature of the instance – it cannot have a definition. Concepts have definitions, but instances do not. Every individual human being shares the attributes of humanity, and humanity has a definition. But none of us individual human beings has a definition. We will return to how this can be justified later.

However, once again, it is not quite as simple as that for data management. We need to keep all the records straight in our database tables. We discover problems such as the accidental duplication of personal records. John Doe might be represented by two records in the database at his doctor's office because his personal data was independently input on two different occasions. How can we figure out that both apply to John Doe? The answer comes from the fact that there can be a description of John Doe. John Doe shares all the attributes of a human, but these attributes are not fixed in any instance – they have determinations. John Doe will have a particular determination of gender, age, height, weight, and so on. All humans share these attributes but John Doe has one particular combination of how they are expressed, and it is though these that we can recognize John Doe. Thus John Doe has a description, not a definition, that allows us to recognize his identity.

Putting Term, Concept, and Instance Together

The term, the concept, and the instance all fit together. Figure 4.1 provides a very abbreviated example of how this works. There is a lot more to it, of course, and even today we do not have a clear understanding of exactly how the human mind processes information. Luckily, we need be concerned only about the results of the processing, not the mechanics.

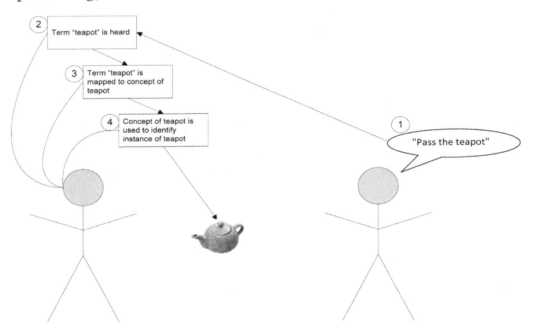

Figure 4.1: *Interaction of Term, Concept, and Instance*

In Figure 4.1, the term "teapot" is heard by the listener. The word "teapot" is simply a sign or label that by convention in the English language identifies the concept of the teapot. The listener understands this and also has a clear concept of a teapot.

A teapot has a globular body, an "S"-shaped spout for pouring tea, a handle, a removable lid, and so on. Its purpose is to permit the infusion of tea leaves into a contained body of hot water. The listener also knows that the speaker expects the listener to identify the same concept. Because the listener identifies the concept to which the speaker refers, the speaker can search for and identify the object referenced. The listener then passes the teapot to the speaker.

What is interesting is that the term "teapot" is first referenced as a concept in the listener's mind, and only after that is it related to the actual object. A term signifies a concept, and a concept is related to an instance.

This illustrates the critical nature of definitions. A concept is not simply a mental picture. It is supported by an understanding of a composite nature that comprises the attributes of that nature. This understanding of the concept, when formally stated, is the basis of its definition. However, there are still many more aspects to be considered when making and using definitions.

Finally, Figure 4.2 attempts to provide a higher level illustration of the general environment in which definitions are found. The reader should be warned that this is merely a preliminary attempt and that much of what is shown has been debated for centuries. Nevertheless, we are obliged to try to show ways in which data may fit with what it is supposed to represent. Current models should be considered straw men that can be criticized in order to arrive at a better understanding. No doubt future advances will provide a clearer picture. (See Fig. 4.2, page 58.)

Definiendum and Definiens

It is also necessary to say something of the structure of definitions. Technically, a definition consists of at least two parts. The *definiendum* is the term to be defined. Interestingly, the *definiendum*

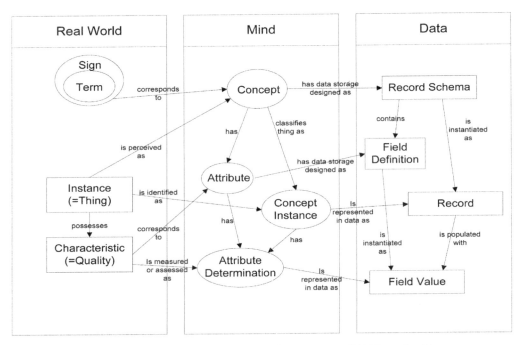

Figure 4.2: *Preliminary Illustration of Data and What It Represents*

always seems to be stated to be a term (i.e., a word or phrase) in the literature about definitions, rather than as some other kind of sign. As data management encounters more requirements for processing images, it is possible that such signs may become more important. A possible example is naval silhouettes that identify classes of vessel. However, we will confine ourselves to *definienda* that are terms, because these are the overwhelming majority today.

The *definiens* is the text and/or images that provide the definition of the *definiendum*. Obviously, this is the major focus when trying to manage definitions.

At this point, we have covered the basic elements of what goes into a definition. Now we can look briefly at the role definitions have played in the history of thought, and how the theory of definitions has been developed over time.

The Early Greek View of Definitions

Western science and philosophy have been greatly influenced by the ancient Greeks. By about 700 - 600 B.C., Greek civilization was thinking deeply about the physical universe. A couple of hundred years later, the focus had shifted to the mind. One reason for this shift was that the Greeks developed a considerable understanding of geometry, through the contribution of such individuals as Pythagoras. They noticed that in geometry there were ideal shapes, like triangles and squares, which never occur perfectly in nature. They felt that concepts could be similarly understood: they do not exist in the real world, but yet represent instances in the real world that do exist. Furthermore, mathematicians like Pythagoras were able to deduce properties of a shape such as a triangle from a very few pieces of information about the shape. This was the so-called axiomatic method that generated logical proofs within geometry. Just a few foundational starting points could be used to figure out everything else in broad areas of geometry. These starting points were felt by the Greeks to be *essential characteristics*, and represented the definitions of geometric figures.

This revolution in thought then proceeded to carry the Greeks away. They decided that if they could find the essential characteristics of any concept – its definition – then by logical proofs they could figure out every other property of that concept. If it worked in geometry, and if mathematics turns out to underlie everything, then why should this approach not work more widely?

Greek philosophers began to turn from questions about nature to questions about the mind. The first great exemplar of using definitions to deduce further knowledge was Socrates. Socrates decided that he knew nothing, but that he might be able to get definitions of things from other people. He would waylay his fellow Athenians in the street and ask them if they could give him definitions of truth, justice, virtue, and so on. He was asking for definitions strong enough to support a superstructure of logical proofs, just as in geometry. When his unfortunate neighbors proceeded to expound, Socrates would quickly come up with further questions. This approach usually resulted in the interrogated person feeling compelled to admit to the same level of ignorance as Socrates on the matter at hand. The required definitions were never found, at least for the very important concepts. This pursuit of clarity in areas like morality and politics eventually annoyed the Athenians so much that Socrates was obliged to commit suicide.

Aristotle and His Followers

Aristotle, who lived about a century after Socrates, took Greek philosophy to new heights. His interests were very broad, but perhaps his single greatest achievement was the foundation of formal logic. He wrote six books on the subject that were later grouped into a collection called the Organon. Aristotle's logic was not simply abstract philosophy; it was also intended to be of broad practical use in human life. It dominated Western and Middle Eastern thought for centuries and exercises enormous influence today.

Aristotle made a major contribution to definitions within the framework of his logic. He formalized the idea that the purpose of a definition is to capture the essence of something, and he proposed a method of using logical division to arrive at definitions.

Aristotle's ideas on definitions were refined and better explained by his followers. A particularly important contribution was made by Porphyry, a Neoplatonist philosopher who lived in the third century A.D. He wrote a commentary on Aristotle that included a diagrammatic representation of the process of logical division. It is shown in Figure 4.3.

The traditional content of the Tree of Porphyry, shown here, is not the topic at hand. Trees of Porphyry can be constructed for many different topic areas. What matters is the process of logical

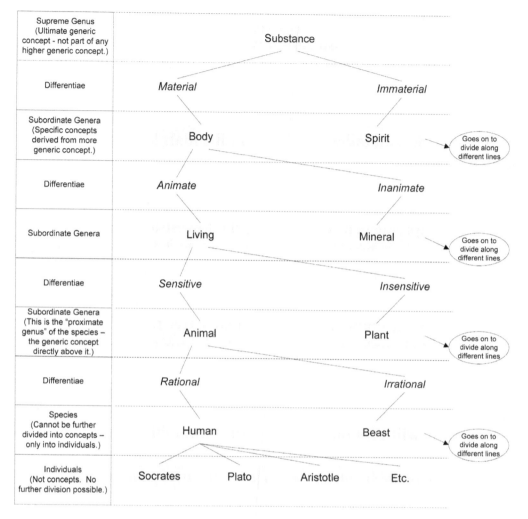

Figure 4.3: *The Tree of Porphyry*

division that it illustrates, which Porphyry owed to Aristotle, and how it can be applied to definitions. The tree shows that it is possible to split a **generic concept** (the "genus") up into two or more **specific concepts** (the "species"). Today we would call a "genus" a "class" or a "set," but we will use the original terminology here.

The Tree of Porphyry was taught as a logical method for centuries, and was common in elementary texts on logic up until about the beginning of the 20th century. Today, we associate the terms

61

"genus" and "species" with biology and not with logic. But the system of biological classification was based on Aristotle's theory of logical division, from which its terms are derived.

It begins at the top with a "supreme genus" or "category." That is a concept that cannot be derived from any other concept. It ends at the bottom with individuals. The individuals belong to the most specific concept that can be derived in the whole tree. This lowest-level specific concept cannot be divided into further concepts, so it is where the process of logical division stops. Within the tree, below the supreme genus and above the lowest-level species, each generic concept is examined to see if it can be broken into subordinate generic concepts ("subordinate genera"). There are a number of rules for doing this, to keep the whole tree consistent.

Of course, the content of any particular tree generally depends on its intended application. We can take motor vehicles as a "supreme genus" and divide up the concept until we get to the lowest level specific concepts. Or perhaps we can begin with financial asset classes and see how they break down. Perhaps financial asset classes will contain a concept for automobile leases, which suggests that relationships can exist between different trees. However, here we begin to stray from our interest in logical division, which is its relevance to definitions.

What the Tree of Porphyry did for definitions was to provide a visual guide for the formation of definitions. It was felt that the species at the same level (the "coordinate species") each had a specific difference from one another, within a uniform basis of division used to divide the genus from which they were derived. Thus "animal" got divided into "human" and "beast" based on rationality – humans being rational animals and beasts being irrational animals. "Rational" and "irrational" are therefore the specific differences in this example. The specific difference(s) – "differentia" (plural "differentiae") – became very important in definitions.

Thus, the logicians used logical division to divide up concepts and held that the definition of anything was the genus from which it derived plus its specific differences. In other words:

$$\text{Definition} = \text{Superordinate Genus} + \text{Differentia(e)}$$

$$\text{E.g., Human} = \text{Rational animal}$$

Humans belong to the superordinate genus "animal," but they are different from other animals in that they are rational.

It was hoped that the differentiae would somehow be the essential characteristics in which the ancient Greeks had placed so much faith. Irrespective of how well placed that faith was, Aristotle's use of logical division to produce definitions was a powerful methodology that could produce practical results. It was a road map for how to get to definitions.

This view of definition pervaded the work of the medieval logicians and remained a basic part of traditional logic until it disappeared from its former prominent position in the public educational systems of the West in the decades preceding World War I.

Definitions in Modern Times

Modern philosophy seems to see logic as more of an area for academic research than, as in former times, a tool or art that could address the everyday problems of ordinary people. Logic today, including the logic of definition, seems to focus on symbolic systems that appear detached from normal experience, and perhaps from reality. There is a wide use of highly technical language and it is almost impossible to find simple explanations of what it represents. Perhaps some of these technical terms are merely synonyms for more widely known ones.

A second focus is on words rather than things, or concepts. This is termed "semantics" and is strongly related to the study of language, or linguistics. There is undoubtedly much value in this focus. For instance, natural language processing (NLP) can provide value to some enterprises, as well as being of academic interest in its own right.

When it comes to definitions of things, or concepts, there seems to be less interest. Indeed, many modern philosophers have denied that things can have definitions, and claim that only words can. This view was certainly enunciated by J. S. Mill in the middle of the 19th century. Judging from the difficulty in finding current academic work on the definitions of things, his view appears to prevail today. In terms of broader logic, where there is any focus on things rather than symbols, the things considered are often the material things relevant to natural science. Indeed, the focus is not even really on the things themselves, but on the relationships among them. This evolution of thought can be traced in a list of famous definitions of the term "definition" presented in *Appendix 4*.

In my experience, modern symbolic logic is not generally used in data management, or even related disciplines such as business analysis. However, people working in these disciplines are constantly hungering after more reliable guides for their work. Communicating the true meaning of things through definitions is a major need, but, unfortunately, modern philosophy seems to have little or nothing practical to offer. Instead it seems confined to circles of academics who pursue controversies of their own making among themselves.

Five

Data and Metadata Objects Requiring Definitions

oncepts require definitions, but we are still stuck with the fact that terms signify concepts. And in data management we find terms used to label data in many different kinds of places. The practical question then arises as to whether it is worthwhile to provide definitions for the concepts that lie behind the terms found in each of these kinds of places. If the concept behind each term is identical in all the places where the term appears, then there can be no need to modify definitions depending on where these terms are found. But is this really the case? If it is not, then the concept signified by a term may subtly vary depending on where the term is used, and we will need to factor this variation into the management of definitions.

It is also worth thinking about the kinds of places where definitions may be needed to set the scope of work needed in definition management. Perhaps some of these locations are of more interest to the enterprise than others. Perhaps there are dependencies among them that will dictate the sequence in which definition management needs to be carried out.

Types of Data and Metadata Objects

There are two main types of places where terms that label data can be found:

- **Data objects.** These are artifacts that store data or present data in some way.

- **Metadata objects.** These are artifacts relevant to the analysis, design, and management of information systems. Typically, they are found where data structures and content are planned for, designed, or documented.

Each of these types of object can be further subdivided into types of object that are found in enterprises. Table 5.1 shows the most usual subdivisions for data objects, together with the containers that normally house these objects.

Data Object Container	Data Object	Summary Definition of Data Object
Database	Table	A way of storing data where rows (records) usually represent individual things and columns usually represent characteristics that all the things represented have in common.
Database	Column	A way to store data that represents the existence of a particular characteristic in a thing or the determination of a characteristic in an individual thing.
Application	Screen	A display in a given physical medium that can be refreshed and shows data to the user.
Application	Screen Label	A fixed text on a screen that is a term used to describe one or more data values that are presented next to or close to it.

Data Object Container	Data Object	Summary Definition of Data Object
Application	Report	A presentation of data values in a form that is fixed. Traditionally, reports were printed on paper. More recently, reports are electronic files. A report is a snapshot of data that does not change.
Application	Report Label	A text on a report that describes an item or grouping of data.
Application	Interface File	A set of data that is a package used to move data from one data store to another.

Table 5.1: *Common Types of Data Object*

Table 5.2 shows the subdivisions for metadata objects, together with the containers that normally house these objects.

Metadata Object Container	Metadata Object	Summary Definition of Metadata Object
Enterprise Glossary	Business Concept	A concept that applies to the enterprise without any element of information management in it.
Data Model	Entity Type	A type of thing of interest to the enterprise that is documented in a data model intended to design a database table.
Data Model	Attribute	A characteristic of a type of thing of interest to the enterprise that is documented in a data model intended to lead to the design of a column of a table in a database.

Metadata Object Container	Metadata Object	Summary Definition of Metadata Object
Data Model	Relationship	An association of two entity types in a data model via attributes they share. A relationship is usually intended to lead to the design of a rule for synchronizing data values in the shared columns in the database tables. Such rules are often enforced through program logic.

Table 5.2: *Summary of Metadata Objects*

Tables 5.1 and 5.2 are not intended to be complete, and there may be many other types of data and metadata object that should be considered with respect to definitions. Even for the items listed in the table, there are many additional considerations than are provided in the summary definitions. However, the types listed in Tables 5.1 and 5.2 are frequently encountered in the information management architectures of all enterprises, and thus need thinking about for the purposes of definition management.

Although the data objects are the most familiar and important in information management, the metadata objects are logically prior to them, so we will consider the metadata objects first.

Types of Metadata Objects

During the analysis and design phases of the construction of databases, it is necessary to model the data objects that will eventually be built. Regrettably, many databases are built with little design. At best, these databases tend to be documented after implementation, and the resulting documentation is frequently of poor quality. Nevertheless, even if metadata objects are based on *post facto* documentation, they are very important for definitions. Let us now examine them in detail.

Business Concept

A business concept is supposed to be a type of thing that the business is interested in, without any reference to computerized systems. In the early days of computing, it referred to a type of thing for which information management was to be automated. Today, many business analysts still seek this purity and try to get the subject matter experts (SMEs) to define business concepts in ways that totally exclude any reference to computerization. This is a major challenge for definitions because in many cases the SMEs have no experience of how the business concepts exist abstracted from the computerized applications that manage them.

This problem has severe ramifications. It should first be understood that attempts by business analysts to exclude references to computerization have a strong foundation. If computer applications can be excluded successfully, then the definition of a business concept will not prejudice the design of any proposed new application. This is in line with the best thinking in business process re-engineering. Michael Hammer warned against "paving the cowpath" in his book *Re-engineering the Corporation*. But when concepts can be understood only in the context of a current implementation, then any new implementation will likely look just like the old one. A common result in IT is "technical conversions," where old applications are simply replaced by clones in more updated technologies, with few, if any, process improvements. This is "paving the cowpath." It is true that such technologies often scale better and often interoperate with other parts of an IT infrastructure. However, these advantages often hide the fact that, from a business perspective, nothing has really changed. If a process was poorly designed prior to the technical conversion, it will be unchanged after the conversion, and an opportunity has been lost. When the business needs to change, it may be impossible to understand, let alone modify, the processes involved. Thus, IT architectures often cannot evolve at the speed the business demands, despite the mirage of progress that adopting new technology creates. This root problem of not being able to get to the business concept is essentially one of definition, and it is quite difficult to appreciate. Even so, it is reasonable to suspect that the costs to enterprises are enormous, varying from loss of efficiency to putting the survival of the enterprise itself at risk.

Analysis is both art and science, but is more of an art. And it is not undemanding. Definitions of business concepts may have to be captured with great difficulty, rather than simply gathered with ease. However, abstracting away from current implementations to find out what the enterprise is really trying to do is undeniably essential. Therefore, while a study of analysis is beyond the scope of this book, the reader will doubtless appreciate that definitions for business concepts are driven by different needs from definitions for other types of data object, and that definitions for business concepts can be of enormous value.

Entity Type

An entity type is typically seen in a graphical logical data model. A logical data model is part analysis and part design; it shows the data the enterprise manages as it should appear to the enterprise. For instance, an enterprise may have to have knowledge of countries (a business concept). In a logical data model, the business concept of **Country** might be implemented via an entity type that has a *Country Code* and a *Country Name* taken from the ISO-3166 alpha-2 standard.

From this it can be seen that the element of design adds something to the definition of the business concept alone. Why is the enterprise choosing the ISO-3166 alpha-2 standard? The answer should be included in the definition. How does the enterprise become aware of changes in the ISO-3166 alpha-2 standard? The answer should be included in the definition. How are exceptions to the ISO-3166 alpha-2 standard to be dealt with? The answer should be included in the definition. And so on.

Entity types in logical data models are also more detailed and precise than business concepts. We may have a single business concept such as **Customer,** but in a logical data model it may turn into many entities. Perhaps this is because customers go through an on-boarding process that has various stages such as "Unqualified Lead," "Qualified Lead," "Pending Conversion," "Active Customer," "Former Customer." A new entity type called **Customer Lifecycle Status** may need to be created to hold the information about these states. Thus, aspects of the business concept of **Customer** may correspond to many logical entity types. This correspondence affects definitions, and we should expect that one business concept may correspond to many entity types.

Simply copying the definition from a business concept to an entity type is therefore likely to miss a good deal of definitional information. Unfortunately, this happens all too often. The prevailing idea tends to be that data definitions include only what the data is trying to represent, not how it is trying to represent it.

Attribute

Attributes correspond to the characteristics of types of things. For example, an individual customer will have a gender and a birth date. Such characteristics are often not included in business concepts. However, they must be fully documented in a logical data model.

Attributes belong to entity types. It can be difficult to produce a high-quality definition for an attribute if there is little to say about it. In these cases, there is often a tendency to make attribute definitions tautological. For instance, the attribute *Customer Key* could be defined as

a key that uniquely identifies a Customer

Such a definition is not very helpful. It could have been easily deduced from the term "Customer Key." It says nothing about how the key value is assigned. Is the value a random number or a sequential number? If sequential, does it conceal other information like the order in which contracts are signed with customers? Such a definition says nothing about any intelligence in the key value. Very often, there is such intelligence – for example, customer keys that begin with "077" represent employees. Many more such questions could be asked that the above definition may not address.

Another problem with attribute definitions is that they may overlap with the definition of the entity type to which they belong. This is particularly true of attributes whose determinations may uniquely (or near uniquely) identify instances of the entity type. These are termed "key attributes" or "alternate keys" or "candidate keys." There are differences between these types of key which space does not allow us to explore here, but the key point is that the definition of the entity type may describe what can be used to uniquely identify it. This information may be repeated in the definitions of the corresponding attributes. We now have a situation where definitions may be inconsistent, or even contradictory. Further, there is also a management issue of needing to update definitions in more than one place, if such updates are necessary,

A good way to approach this problem is to keep all definitions for attributes associated with the attributes themselves, and not in the definition of the entity type to which they refer. It should also be remembered that data modeling tools are often sophisticated enough to identify primary keys, alternate keys, and candidate keys. If a data modeling tool keeps such structured metadata, there should be no need to repeat it in the definition. Repetition would introduce a management problem and a risk to consistency.

Relationship

Relationships are extremely important in data modeling, but regarding their definitions they often receive little attention.

One reason is that a relationship does not always represent a thing, and there is often an absolute presupposition among analysts that only types of things can have a definition.

Secondly, many data modeling tools allow a "verb phrase" to be entered for a relationship. A "verb phrase" is really only a construct that allows us to form a term to signify the relationship, and very often the significance is trivial. For instance, suppose we have a data model where there is a relationship between the entity type **Customer** and the entity type **Customer Address.** The analyst may document the verb phrase as "lives at." This allows a reader to state the relationship as "Customer lives at Customer Address," which is no doubt useful, but is not a definition.

However, there can be much more information about a relationship, which the following example illustrates. Suppose we have an entity type of **Customer** and every **Customer** can have a **Customer Mailing Address** and a **Customer Billing Address.** Figure 5.1 shows how this could be modeled with distinct entity types for the two different types of address, simply using "has" for the verb phrase. (See Fig. 5.1, page 74.)

In this design we could specify the nature of each type of address in the two entity types **Customer Mailing Address** and **Customer Billing Address** respectively. However, this design may not be the best for the enterprise. Figure 5.2 shows an alternative design. Here, a single entity type, **Customer Address,** is not dependent on **Customer** as in Figure 5.1. (See Fig. 5.2, page 74.)

Here the **Customer Address** entity can represent addresses that are not as yet linked with a **Customer.** More important, one address can be used as a billing address, or a mailing address or

Customer Mailing Address

Customer Mailing Address Sequence Number Customer Key (FK)
Customer Mailing Address Line 1 Customer Mailing Address Line 2 Customer Mailing Address City Customer Mailing Address State Customer Mailing Address Zip Code

Customer

Customer Key
Customer First Name Customer Last Name

—has—

Customer Billing Address

Customer Billing Address Sequence Number Customer Key (FK)
Customer Billing Address Line 1 Customer Billing Address Line 2 Customer Billing Address City Customer Billing Address State Customer Billing Address Zip Code

—has—

Figure 5.1: *Data Model Fragment for Customer with Explicit Mailing and Billing Addresses*

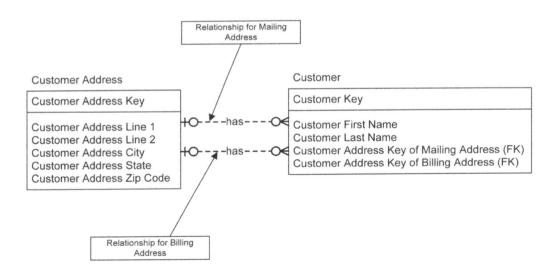

Figure 5.2: *Unique Addresses and Many Relationships for Customer and Address*

both. In this design we must store the definition of what a billing address or mailing address is in either

(a) the respective relationships between **Customer** and **Customer Address** or

(b) the migrated foreign key attributes in **Customer,** that is *Customer Address Key of Mailing Address* and *Customer Address Key of Billing Address.*

Since we have already shown that it is not desirable to define more than the attribute in an attribute definition, we can eliminate the second option and conclude that in this design the definitions of *Customer Mailing Address* and *Customer Billing Address* belong in the relationships.

This example illustrates that it is important to consider definitions for relationships, and that sometimes non-trivial definitions will be necessary for relationships.

Table

With tables we pass from metadata to what is generally termed "physical" data, although in reality, there is no such thing as physical data – it is all patterns in storage media that acquire meaning only through interpretation.

Tables in relational databases are ideally direct implementations of entities in logical data models. This ideal rarely occurs in practice. Considerations such as performance, ease of programming, or ease of navigation may make the design of a table quite different from any entity types on which it is based.

Therefore, we have also passed more decisively from the realm of analysis into the realm of design. Table definitions should contain information on the design decisions and why these decisions were made. If we go back to only defining the thing the table represents, we will never understand what happened during the design of the table. Once again, we see that the duality of data – what it represents and the data itself – must be reflected in definitions.

Entity types in logical data models are typically a lot "purer" than tables in databases in that the latter often represent more than one concept. Unless this is explicitly stated in the definition of the table, it will be very difficult to find out. Finally, the content of tables very much depends on how the users use them. There is nothing to stop a user using a table for purposes other than for which it was intended. This too should be documented in the definition if it is discovered.

Again, therefore, we see that tables as data objects have definitional requirements that differ from entity types and business concepts.

Column

Just as tables should ideally implement entity types, so columns in database tables should ideally implement attributes. It is probably fair to say that attributes are less distorted in databases than entity types are, and so we can expect a much closer relationship between the definition for an attribute and the definition for a column.

However, this is true only prior to the users beginning to work with the databases. There is nothing to stop users from putting data content into a column that does not match the definition of the column, nor of the attribute on which it is based. If such misuse is detected, the column definition will need to be updated to reflect the true state of affairs – unless such misuse can be reversed, which is rare. Thus we can conclude that columns too may have their unique definitional requirements.

Screen

Screens are used for the display and entry of data. Definitions of screens will be most useful to those who design the screens and those who use them. However, this immediately raises the question of the need for distinct definitions for screens. After all, are screens not described in specifications written for the people that build them, and user guides for the people that use them?

This may indeed be true, but it is still worthwhile thinking about definitions for screens. Enterprises rarely keep any kind of inventory of their data objects, and so there is typically no central list of all the screens in all the applications of an enterprise. Oddly, physical inventories of tables, chairs, filing cabinets, and the like exist, but they are much rarer for data objects. If an enterprise wanted to set up such an inventory, then it must provide a definition of a screen so that anyone consulting the inventory could understand what the screen is intended for. The alternative would be to go looking for the appropriate documentation in the specifications and user guides for the myriad of applications in the enterprise. Such an approach is expensive, not scalable, and must be repeated every time the same question is asked.

It is difficult to persuade executive management of the value of maintaining an inventory of screens. Why they can understand the need for an inventory that will include a chair worth less than one hundred dollars but dismiss the need for an inventory to include a screen that cost tens of thousands of dollars to develop is difficult to comprehend. Yet at the same time they complain of runaway costs in IT, while accepting the need to employ large numbers of analysts who are mostly trying to understand what IT has done in the past.

It is also fairly rare for screens to be uniquely identified by a single term or identifier. That is an immediate problem for definitions, because without such a term or identifier, it will be difficult for anyone to figure out which screen a definition applies to.

Nevertheless, a few enterprises have attempted to implement inventories of screens. The definitions for each screen often involve aspects of the intended use of the screen, screen navigation, and high level rules, some of which may include manual procedures. This indicates that screens have definitions in their own right with their own unique requirements.

Screen Label

A screen label is a term that appears on a screen, usually next to a data entry field that it refers to, or a pure displayed data item. Ideally, a screen label describes a column from a database. Given this, it should be possible to use the same definition as the definition for the column.

Of course, the terms used for labels on screens may not be the same as those used for columns or attributes, but this does not mean that the concepts are different. Alternate terms can simply be managed as synonyms and point to common definitions. This is perhaps the most urgent need when dealing with screens.

However, not all labels on screens describe data. They may refer to actions, such as labels for buttons. The screen labels that do not correspond to data items in an underlying database still require definitions.

The need to manage definitions for screen labels outside of user guides is much less clear than the need to manage an inventory of screens. The enterprises that manage such an inventory are often concerned with impact analysis – the need to know where on screens a database column is used. However, the definition of the underlying column would seem to be enough, and in impact analysis there is no need to track the screen labels that do not refer to an underlying column. Thus it seems that screen labels may be questionable candidates for definition management, but no doubt there are exceptions to this.

Report

Much of what was said about screens can be said of reports, with one important difference. Reports often filter the data they present to the user. One of the vital needs for report definitions is to describe where the data came from. A vast swathe of shadow applications exists in most enterprises where users keep their own spreadsheets and other files to check what appears on the reports they get from IT applications. High quality definitions for all reports could go a long way to rectifying this situation. If a user could always be certain what data appeared on a report, a good deal of wasted resources could be saved.

Another reason to provide definitions for all reports is the vast number of reports that typically exist in an enterprise but are not used. It often seems that the only reports that are actually used are those that have been developed rather recently or have some pedigree that means that they received a lot of attention. The savings that could come from eliminating unused reports are occasionally so obvious that special projects are started for the purpose. It would be simpler to understand the reports that exist in the enterprise and what they do.

That said, it is the filtering of data that is the most unique aspect of reports and the aspect that should be put into their definitions.

Report Label

Report labels usually do the same work as screen labels, and it might be thought that, in general, there is little need to define them. Often this is true, but once again there is a major exception. Reports often include calculations and derivations. These may be as simple as column totals, which are fairly obvious; they may also be more complex.

When we have a derivation or computation in a report, we are essentially dealing with a new attribute, and sometimes a new business concept. All the reasons for maintaining definitions of business concepts and attributes thus apply to derived and computed items in reports. An added difficulty is that there will probably be no pre-existing definition for any other data or metadata object that the report label can inherit with modification. Thus, the scope of the definition required for a report label for a derived or computed field may be quite broad.

A further complication is that what is assumed to be the same computed or derived data is often independently computed or derived in many reports. Issues of consistency can arise from this, and consistency issues are often the biggest headaches in dealing with reports. One solution is to implement the derivations or computations in the underlying database as new columns. In the cases where this cannot be done, the need for definitions of report labels is overwhelming.

Interface File

Interface files move data from one location to another. They are always created in response to a specific requirement. Once again, it may be argued that specifications are enough to maintain all the knowledge of an interface file. However, the set of point-to-point data transfers that exist in an enterprise can be fully understood only when there is an inventory of them, which is rare. If an inventory is ever developed, it becomes obvious that definitions are needed, and the arguments used in the cases of screens and reports apply.

The unique aspects of interface files that need management would include the business reasons for their existence, the source(s) and target(s) involved, timing issues, and so on. Often data must be transformed to be placed in an interface file, and these transformations need to be captured too. Because of this, individual fields in an interface file may need their own definitions. A further issue is that the file exists to move data from a source to a target, and very often each is the responsibility of a different organization. Each organization must agree to the definitions of the components of the file. This is a governance issue, and it may impact the definitions. For instance, until both organizations fully agree with a definition, it may need to be flagged with a special status.

Perhaps a good deal of definitional information for interface files can come from the source columns used. Other information can be made into structured metadata outside of definitions – for example, the sources and targets. Yet a residue will nearly always remain that should be part of a definition.

Conclusion

This survey of common types of data objects and metadata objects shows that there are valid reasons for providing definitions for most of them, and most of them also have unique definitional requirements. This approach argues strongly against a single definition for one type of data object as all that is required in an enterprise.

Yet difficulties remain. IT professionals tend to focus on projects rather than sustainable activities. So a typical reaction to the conclusions presented above might be to wonder whether the enterprise can afford to sponsor a project to go out and "do definitions for everything." The answer is that it almost certainly could not. But that is not the only option. A better option is to think carefully about data governance and then set up processes and supporting infrastructure to capture definitions on an ongoing basis. At a minimum, such a project should aim to greatly reduce, if not eliminate, analyst rework in which the same questions about definitions are repeatedly asked, and require repeated, redundant analysis, because the information gathered each time is not stored anywhere.

Furthermore, not all types of data and metadata objects must be tackled immediately. An enterprise could focus on one or a few at a time. This is a better approach than trying to do too much at one time. What is most important to understand, however, is

- There are not vague "things" that need definitions, but rather clearly different types of data and metadata objects.

- A definition for one type of data or metadata object may not meet all the requirements expected of a definition for another type, so definitions are not always fully interchangeable.

It should be understood that enterprises may have additional data and metadata objects that are different from those discussed here. In the future, new technologies may introduce even more. Enterprises need to decide which types of data and metadata objects they will maintain definitions for, and think about how these are related.

Real Versus Nominal Definitions

We have looked at the role of definitions, the basic theory and history of definitions, the reasons for having definitions, and where definitions should be applied. We now start to examine procedures for high-quality definitions in data management.

Perhaps the first thing to appreciate is that there are two distinct kinds of definitions. The question is, therefore, whether such a division is relevant to data management, and if so, how it applies to the practicalities of data management.

The two major kinds of definition are

- **Real definition.** This kind of definition fully explains the nature of a concept. It goes beyond providing awareness that something exists, to tell us what it is.

- **Nominal definition.** Explains the meaning of a word or term. For example, the word "thunder" could be defined as "a noise in the clouds." This gives us enough information to know what the word "thunder" refers to, but it does not tell us much about what thunder really is.

Aristotle seems to have been the first to recognize the two kinds of definition. For millennia, logicians and other thinkers have tried to grapple with the difficulties raised by the division. For instance, Dr. Samuel Johnson wrote:

> I am not yet so lost in lexicography, as to I forget that WORDS ARE THE DAUGHTERS OF EARTH, AND THAT THINGS ARE THE SONS OF HEAVEN. Language is only the instrument of science, and words are but the signs of ideas: I wish, however, that the instrument might be less apt to decay, and that signs might be permanent, like the things which they denote. [Preface to a Dictionary of the English Language, 1755.]

This statement, from the author of the first widely used English dictionary, is a striking illustration of the gulf that exists between nominal and real definitions.

Modeling the Types of Definition

If we are to understand the relevance of nominal and real definitions for data management, it is probably a good idea to try to understand them using data management techniques. Figure 6.1 is a cartoon that illustrates the two kinds of definition.

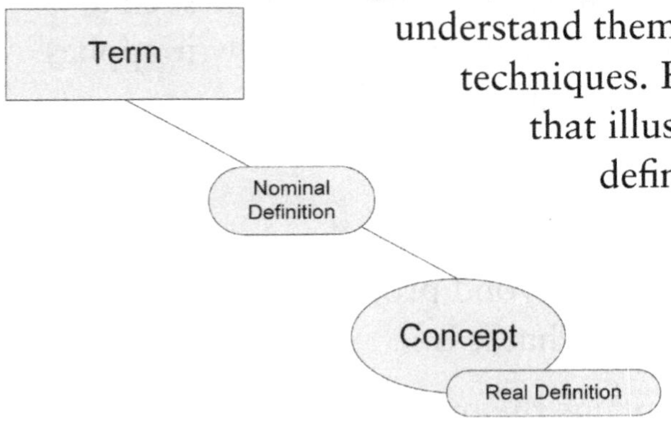

Figure 6.1 *Real and Nominal Definition*

Let us start with "term" in Figure 6.1. Terms are composed of words, and words are symbols, that is, signs. They represent something else. If a spoken word did not represent something else it would be a meaningless sound. Thus a term has meaning. This meaning is the identification of the concept that the term refers to, and is thus an attribute of the relation between the term and that concept. The meaning is the nominal definition. Since there are far more concepts than words, we often use the same words to signify different things. In such cases one term has many nominal definitions, but between one term and one concept there can be only one nominal definition. A term cannot have zero nominal definitions.

Yet the concept itself has a stable definition that is not dependent on the terms that may signify it. This is the real definition. It is not dependent on the nominal definitions of the terms that signify it. If there really were such a definition, we would all be in trouble due to the fact that language evolves. For instance, the word "presently" used only to mean what we today understand by "currently" or "right now." Today it more commonly means "soon" or "in the near future." The concepts we understand by (a) "currently," and (b) "soon" exist independently of how we use the word "presently" and the two concepts have their own real definitions. The problem (or set of problems) for human beings is that we must label concepts by terms, and terms have an uncontrollable tendency to change their nominal definitions. Meanwhile concepts have definitions that fundamentally do not change, but which we can come to know better or worse over time.

If we try to put Figure 6.1. into a data model, we arrive at the illustration in Figure 6.2:

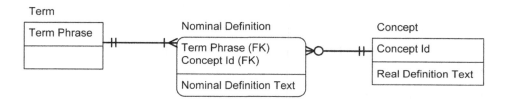

Figure 6.2: *Data Model Fragment for Real and Nominal Definitions*

Thus we see that a **Term** has a primary key, which is the word or phrase that composes the term. A **Concept** can be uniquely identified only by some kind of surrogate key, such as a number, because there is no one-to-one correspondence between **Term** and **Concept** – because of the problem of homonyms. **Nominal Definition** is an association entity between **Term** and **Concept** that resolves the underlying many-to-many relationship between **Term** and **Concept.**

Interestingly, a **Term** must be associated with one or more **Nominal Definitions**, but a **Concept** need not be. It may not be related to any nominal definitions at all. This makes sense if we have concepts for which we do not yet have terms. Such concepts can be described only by their real definitions, although the real definition may initially be little better than any nominal definition. Such circumstances occur in data management when analysts realize that a concept exists but are unsure what terms are used to name it.

Turning to the relevant attributes in Figure 6.2, *Nominal Definition Text* in **Nominal Definition** must be populated. If it were null, we would have a **Term** with no **Nominal Definition.** Of course, in real world circumstances, it might take some time to collect the nominal definition, and for this period the attribute would be null. However, we can be sure in the meantime that some version of *Nominal Definition Text* does exist.

This is more or less also true for the *Real Definition Text* attribute in the **Concept** entity. It may initially be the same as the *Nominal Definition Text*, but as a particular concept becomes better defined, the content of *Real Definition Text* should go far beyond *Nominal Definition Text*. Philosophers might add that there are concepts that no humans know about, just as relativity existed before Einstein. However, it is impossible to manage a specific concept of which we are unaware, so while this problem may be relevant to philosophy, we need not worry about it in data management.

Validation of Model

It is possible to check the validity of the simple model shown in Figure 6.2. A paper by Alvaro Graves and Claudio Gutierrez offers a diagrammatic representation of sample data in WorldNet, the well-known online dictionary maintained by Princeton University. It is shown in Figure 6.3.

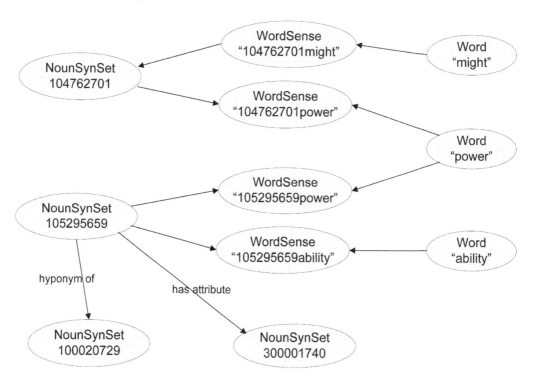

Figure 6.3: *Illustration of Relationships of WordNet Data (after Graves and Gutierrez)*

Obviously, WordNet uses different terminology from that used here. "Synset" appears to mean "concept." There are different classes of "Synsets" – for nouns, verbs, adjectives, and adverbs, "Word" appears to mean "Term," and "WordSense" appears to mean "Nominal Definition." It appears that WordNet uses a surrogate key for "Synsets," e.g., "104762701," just as there was no alternative to a surrogate key to identify instances of **Concept** in Figure 6.2. In WordNet, a "Word" can have one or more "WordSenses," just as a **Term** can have one or more Nominal Definitions in Figure 6.2. Similarly, a "Synset" in WordNet can be associated with one or more "WordSenses," just as a **Concept** is associated with many **Nominal Definitions.**

However, there are also differences. WordNet appears to be focused on nominal definitions, and there is only one type of definition – the text of the definition that appears to be in the "Synset." Nevertheless, the broad outline of what we see in Figure 6.3 seems to support what is contained in Figures 6.1 and 6.2.

Real Versus Nominal Definitions

When the ancient Greeks first considered definitions, they were primarily concerned with real definitions. In modern times many philosophers have denied that real definitions exist at all, and accept only nominal ones. For instance, in the 4th century B.C. Aristotle considered a definition to be "the account of the essence of the thing" [*Topics,* I, 5], whereas in the middle of the 20th century Ludwig Wittgenstein wrote, "Definitions are rules for translating from one language into another. Any correct sign language must be translatable into any other in accordance with such rules: it is this that they all have in common." [*Tractatus Logico–Philosophicus,* Para 3.343]

In data management we are not primarily dealing in words as words. We have created representations of things in order not just to remember facts about these things, but to manipulate the facts we have stored to create other facts that we will ultimately map back to reality. The way we manipulate the stored facts must reflect the ways in which the things they represent actually do behave, or our stores of data will no longer accurately represent reality. Thus we must understand – perhaps only to a certain extent – these things. We must find at least the portions of their real definitions that are relevant to what we are doing with the data that represents them.

Another difference is that nominal definitions are not concerned with how a word, term, or symbol is limited in any way in what it is trying to represent. But this is not true of data, which may have technical constraints that limit its ability to represent things – for example, a maximum length of 80 characters. Perhaps it could be argued that this is somehow not part of real definitions, but it clearly lies closer to real definitions than it does to nominal definitions, and we shall consider it an aspect of real definition here.

Finally, it should be remembered that there is one property that a nominal definition has that a real definition does not. This is its truth value. The use of a nominal definition assumes that people are using the term according to the nominal definition, and this is either true or false. The relevance to data management is important. An analyst recording a nominal definition must ensure that people really are using the term as he is describing it.

Data management, therefore, must focus on real definitions. However, there is still no escape from nominal definitions, and they show up in a variety of ways in data management. The best approach would seem to be to primarily consider real definitions but ensure that any practical problems that relate to nominal definitions are also addressed.

Seven

Seven

Types of Definitions

We have seen that definitions can be split into two main kinds – real and nominal. However, over the centuries, many other types of definition have also been identified. These different types do not necessarily apply either only to real definitions or only to nominal definitions. Nor are the different types of definition mutually exclusive. Rather, they provide a number of alternative ways of approaching the process of producing definitions that an analyst can consider. An analyst might choose one or a combination of them as the approach to creating a particular definition. We will now consider them.

1. Essential Definitions

In the literature of traditional logic, essential definitions are usually represented as the ideal type of definition. They are the type of definitions that ancient Greeks modeled after geometry, and which were discussed in Chapter 4. The Greeks thought that by discovering the essence of a concept, they could deduce everything else about it. The essence was supposed to be the one or few characteristics of the concept that made this deduction possible.

These are supposedly the most precise definitions. They are created by finding the generic concept ("genus") to which the concept under consideration belongs and then identifying the specific ways in which the concept differs from the other concepts that can be split out from the generic concept ("differentia"). This is what we saw diagrammed in Chapter 4 in the Tree of Porphyry. For example, a rectilinear triangle can be defined as

a plane figure contained by three straight lines.

From this we learn that the rectilinear triangle is part of the generic concept "plane figure," and that it is distinguished from other types of plane figure because it comprises three straight lines. Another type of plane figure might be made from four straight lines, and yet another type five straight lines, and so on. From an essential definition such as this it is possible to determine all the other characteristics of the object defined (as Pythagoras did for triangles).

This approach requires that the concept being considered is a specific concept contained in a larger concept. In common data management parlance, it must be part of a "hierarchy." Unfortunately, not everything is part of a hierarchy, but when the concept is, it can work well. Let us consider Bond Credit Ratings. These are generically accepted as consisting of two classes: "Investment Grade" and "High Yield" (sometimes less euphemistically called "Junk"). Suppose we need a definition of "High Yield." The rule to produce the definition is, as discussed in Chapter 4 is traditionally stated as:

Definition = Superordinate Genus + Differentia(e)

We can update the language a little to put it as follows:

To find a definition of a concept

(a) Find the class or set of things to which the concept belongs.

(b) Find the characteristic(s) that the concept has that are different from all the other members of the class or set to which it belongs

(c) Put (a) and (b) together and you have the definition

Returning to our example, we know immediately that the superordinate genus is "Bond Credit Rating." Now we must find the differentiae of "Investment Grade" and "High Yield" within "Bond Credit Rating." One such differentia is the Standard and Poor's rating (at least for long-term bonds) of "BB+." Any bond with a rating of BB+ or worse is "High Yield." Any bond with a rating better than BB+ is "Investment Grade." Thus we can arrive at an initial definition of "High Yield" as

a Bond Credit Rating on the Standard and Poor's scale of BB+ or lower.

However, we must remember that this is only a beginning. The definition must account for other scales besides Standard and Poor's. Further, not everyone always agrees that BB+ is the boundary between "High Yield" and "Investment Grade." And a number of other considerations must appear in the definition. But at least we have a reasonable start.

One other advantage of this technique is that we need not explain anything about what a "Bond Credit Rating" is in the definition of "High Yield." Of course, we must have a separate definition for "Bond Credit Rating" elsewhere. However, the analyst now has a solid rule for limiting the scope of what a definition must explain. Finding such boundaries in analysis is of enormous practical value.

Yet another advantage is that we understand the thing we are defining in terms of at least some of its relationships with other things. The definition of "High Yield" provides an instant understanding of its relationship with "Bond Credit Rating." This too can be very helpful.

However, there are a few problems. The first is the irrelevance of the ancient idea that putting one or a few essential characteristics in a definition allows us to deduce everything else about whatever we are defining. Even if we could do this, which we cannot for most things, it would still be a bad idea. How could we be sure that everyone could perform the deductions? It would be much better to explicitly state everything that can be deduced in the definition.

The second problem is more serious. Not everything fits into a Tree of Porphyry-like hierarchy. Attributes do not. An attribute is a characteristic of an entity type. It is part of a whole and often has no independent existence outside of that whole. And it is sufficiently important, at least for data management, to warrant its own definition. Thus, essential definitions seem to apply to things like entity types. Even then we find problems. What about entity types that are not really part of self-evident hierarchies, like **Party**?

However, there may be imperfect situations where we can still apply the technique with some success. For instance, let us try to form a definition for the concept "country." We must first think of what generic concept "country" is derived from. All the countries make up the world – more or less. There are exceptions like Antarctica which is part of the world, but not a country. Also "the world" does not break down into "country" and other concepts that are not countries – at least not in the same way that"Bond Credit Rating" breaks down into "Investment Grade" and "High Yield." Antarctica is not immediately understood as equivalent to a "country."

The next step is to figure out what differentiates countries from other ways the world could be divided. The world can be divided by geology or geomorphology or ecological zones. What is special about countries is that they are autonomously governed within their political boundaries. However, the geology, geomorphology, ecology, and political units all overlap. Again we do not quite see the clear division we have within "Bond Credit Rating." Even so, thinking how a country differs from other things that are part of the world is helpful, and we can get to an initial definition of "country" as

an autonomously governed area of the world

This is a reasonable start, although a lot more detail must be supplied, and it must deal with possible exceptions such as territories, colonies, regions, and so on. Thus the method of looking for a superordinate genus, even if even if it is not immediately clear, and looking for specific differences, even though there may be exceptions, has been helpful.

2. Distinctive Definitions

A different approach is to form a definition of something by determining its unique characters. This type of definition is called a distinctive definition.

Distinctive definitions have a place in the academic world. They are the kinds of definitions most common in natural science. They list the characteristics of the thing defined. These characteristics are the properties that set the type apart from other types, but they cannot be used to deduce other characteristics of a type, unlike essential definitions (at least in theory).

Ideally, these characteristics will be unique to the concept defined. In fact, any worthwhile definition of a concept must include what is unique to that concept, because we cannot practically expect to find such information anywhere else. Here is a good example of a distinctive definition. It is the definition of "piracy" as defined in the article 101 of the 1982 United Nations Convention on the Law of the Sea (UNCLOS):

Piracy consists of any of the following acts:

(a) any illegal acts of violence or detention, or any act of depredation, committed for private ends by the crew or the passengers of a private ship or a private aircraft, and directed:

(i) on the high seas, against another ship or aircraft, or against persons or property on board such ship or aircraft;

(ii) against a ship, aircraft, persons or property in a place outside the jurisdiction of any State;

(b) any act of voluntary participation in the operation of a ship or of an aircraft with knowledge of facts making it a pirate ship or aircraft;

(c) any act inciting or of intentionally facilitating an act described in sub–paragraph (a) or (b).

[Source: http://www.imo.org/Facilitation/mainframe.asp?topic_id=362, December 2009]

This definition is very descriptive and tells us of the different aspects of piracy and the various elements that make it up.

One error in dealing with distinctive definitions is to limit them to just enough characteristics that an instance can be unambiguously identified as belonging to the concept (or not belonging to the concept). This is very often how distinctive definitions are used in natural science. For instance, a physician trying to diagnose a disease is interested only in the symptomatic characteristics produced by the disease. Doubtless, this works well in medicine, but in an enterprise it is difficult for analysts to predict how data will be utilized, both today and in the future. This suggests that the best method is to make distinctive definitions cover as much ground as possible, and certainly not to confine them to just what is needed for identification, although identification is important.

This again suggests that data is a unique area, and we cannot rely on analogies from other disciplines to tell us how to work with it. Distinctive definitions for data should include everything that is needed to manage the data for a given enterprise. The underlying approach of using distinctive definitions is a good one. In some circumstances, they may be the best we have to work with.

Distinctive definitions also highlight the need for collaboration in their formation. It is easy to see how definitions can be made better over time, by adding details about more characteristics. It is unlikely that one analyst will know about all of the characteristics for a given concept, so many individuals will need to participate in forming the definition.

3. Causal Definitions – Purpose

While distinctive definitions may be a very descriptive approach, sometimes we find concepts for which definitions are not easy to formulate. In these cases, it may be appropriate to include causes in the definition. Causal definitions break down into two kinds: a description of purpose and a description of cause. We will deal with definitions stating a purpose first. For example, Report X123 might be have a definition that begins as follows:

a report requested by the State Insurance Commission summarizing annual insurance premiums in a special format specified by the Commission.

All we know here is that the purpose of the report is to supply a requirement of the State Insurance Commission about premium information. What the Commission does with the report, and why they need it, may be entirely unknown to us.

Describing purposes – what something is for – is very important in many areas of IT. For instance, documentation about the layout and function of data entry screens is often like this. The reader is told what a particular field on a screen "is for" (maybe to enter a Customer's Street Address) or what a particular button "is intended to do" (maybe to save a record). This approach can be taken to such an extreme that the readers complain that they are simply being told "how" to do something without having any explanation of "what" they are dealing with or "why" they are doing it. This is a deficiency of a causal definition because it is not really telling us what something is. On the other hand, it is providing valuable information.

Now, it is also important to realize that there is a major difference between science and data management when it comes to purpose, and this bears directly on our attitude to definitions. Today, scientists actively try to exclude ideas of purpose in the study of the natural world. This was not always so, and the Greeks in particular thought that nature was filled with mind and that things had purpose. These ideas persisted in various forms until they began to be questioned during the Renaissance. Eventually science came to completely abhor the idea of purpose in nature. Thus in the context of modern science, anyone trying to introduce the idea of purpose into definitions will be rapidly denounced. There is a strong possibility that this attitude has affected the way we think of definitions in general.

Unfortunately, data management is not like one of the natural sciences in this respect. While scientists strive to eliminate purpose, data managers need a sense of purpose to understand their work. Everywhere in IT there is an emphasis on the need for strong requirements before doing anything. These requirements tell IT professionals the reasons why something musts be built. They do

not say how to build it – that is the province of the design specifications. When the piece of infrastructure or functionality is built,
it is expected to meet a set of stated requirements – to fulfill their
purpose. It is now generally recognized that undertaking activities
without clear requirements is a recipe for disaster. Furthermore,
it is expected that a link back to the requirements will be made in
all documentation created during the development of a database
or application. This link must be applied to definitions in data
management. Every data store or object where data is presented as
information serves purposes, and wherever possible these purposes
should be included in definitions. The attitude of natural science to
purpose simply does not apply to data management, and the role
of purpose must be recognized in data definitions.

4. Causal Definitions – Cause

A description of the **cause** of the object. For example, Table
ABC might initially be defined as

> *a database table built by the now-disbanded Data
> Warehouse team, whose purpose is unclear.*

Here all we know is something of how the table came into
being, but nothing more. It might be thought that describing the
cause gives the "why," but this is not necessarily the case, as the
above example demonstrates. People nearly always find it helpful
to know why something exists, but there may be a chain of causes.
These causes may be valid, but they tell us nothing about the true
intent behind the concept. For instance, I once came across a very
strange algorithm for assigning surrogate key values and was
told it was simply a standard documented by a certain group in
the enterprise. That was a causal definition. Eventually, I found
out that it had been introduced two decades earlier in order to
distribute head movements over disks to prevent overheating. The
overheating problem was solved by other means within two years

after the algorithm was introduced, but it persisted ever since because any change would have been too expensive. This knowledge, which now included purpose as well as cause, was much better and had the benefit of confirming that there was no technical restriction on selecting a new algorithm in the future.

Obviously, focusing only on purpose and cause is not really a complete answer because they address something other than the nature of the concept we are trying to define. Unfortunately, there are times when we do not know much other than the purpose or the cause.

Including a causal definition as part of a full definition can be very helpful. This is often expressed in IT as "knowing the history behind" something. Even if a concept is fully understood, it may still be difficult to appreciate why instances of it have appeared in an IT infrastructure. Sometimes political decisions may be involved in the chain of events that lead to, say, a particular table or column being added to a database. Although this turn of events perhaps requires some tact, including the information in definitions for future analysts may help them fully grasp why such objects exist. Otherwise the objects may be inexplicable, and analysts may spend a good deal of time trying to find out why they are there.

5. Genetic Definitions

These kinds of definitions are not essential or distinctive, but define something by describing how it is made. Sometimes this is a very good approach. For instance, the best way to understand what a Key Lime Pie is may be to describe how it is made, starting with the ingredients, followed by the method of baking.

In data management we can follow this pattern. For example, a database table in a SQL-compliant relational database could be defined as

a data object made by executing a CREATE statement.

Admittedly this tells us nothing of what a database table is, but it is still a useful piece of definitional information. It should also be remembered that we initially know concepts poorly and get to know them better. Thus, a genetic definition may be the best starting point available. And a genetic definition can be very precise. It can always be supplemented with a more distinctive definition as time goes by.

6. Accidental Definitions

In traditional logic, an "accident" is a characteristic of something that is not part of the true nature of the thing where it is found. For instance, an apple may be red, but a lot of other things are red too. Traditional logic warns us that trying to distinguish things as being truly different based on differing "accidental characters" alone is invalid. The logicians frequently gave the example of using color to divide concepts as an example of meaningless distinction, because color is always an accident and cannot make any difference to the nature of anything.

To some extent, this is the antithesis of the essential definitions discussed earlier. Just as with essential characteristics, "accidental" characteristics can be used to form subclasses of a more general concept, but these subclasses are not thereby guaranteed to be different in their natures. We may end up with distinctions without differences.

Unfortunately, the traditional logicians were often talking about reality, rather than how humans deal with reality. In information management we have the ability to manage as different anything that we choose to be different. If an enterprise feels that it can sell brown eggs for a higher price than white eggs, there is nothing to stop it from assigning a higher price to brown eggs. Yet, scientifically speaking, there is presumably no real difference between brown eggs and white eggs.

It seems therefore that distinctive definitions may need to include "accidents" if the needs of the enterprise so dictate. It is even unclear whether it is worthwhile to distinguish "accidental" characteristics from any other kind. The only test is whether a characteristic is relevant to the enterprise or not.

7. Ostensive Definitions

An ostensive definition is provided simply by showing an example of the thing being defined. For instance, water could be defined by showing someone water in a glass and pointing to it. To some extent, ostensive definitions are a little like nominal definitions. We are in effect saying that the term means "one of those" when we point to "one of those."

This is hardly a useful approach in data management where people are not available to point to things and the definitions must themselves be stored as data. However, it is possible to include a picture or diagram of an example of the thing being defined in the definition. Such an illustration may greatly improve the quality of the definition.

8. Stipulative Definitions

It is possible to make up an entirely new definition for a term that already exists and signifies concepts that have known definitions. This is a stipulative definition. It is also possible that the new concept that the term is now said to signify may already be well defined. The reuse of a term to signify such a concept can be very confusing.

Again, this form of definition seems mostly concerned with nominal definition – the connotation of a word or term being defined rather than the meaning of a concept.

In Lewis Carroll's book *Through the Looking Glass*, Alice and Humpty Dumpty have the following exchange:

"And only *one* for birthday presents, you know. There's glory for you!

"I don't know what you mean by 'glory,'" Alice said.

Humpty Dumpty smiled contemptuously. "Of course you don't – 'till I tell you. I meant 'there's a nice knock–down argument for you!'"

"But 'glory' doesn't mean 'a nice knock–down argument,'" Alice objected.

"When *I* use a word," Humpty Dumpty said in rather a scornful tone, "it means just what I choose it to mean – neither more nor less."

"The question is," said Alice, "whether you *can* make words mean so many different things."

"The question is," said Humpty Dumpty, "which is to be master – that's all."

Lewis Carroll was the pen name of the Reverend Charles Dodgson, a mathematician and logician who taught at Oxford University. His works, ostensibly written for children, contain more about logic than is generally recognized.

Perhaps the best approach is to explicitly recognize that other definitions exist for the term for which a stipulative definition is created. This will at least reduce the risk of confusing a reader, who may otherwise be left wondering if the stipulated definition really differs from one of the traditional definitions associated with the term in question.

9. Legislative Definitions

Stipulative definitions are not always special forms of nominal definitions. There is an important subclass of stipulative definitions that we can term "legislative definitions." Such definitions emerge when we define a concept for the first time, or actually produce a concept for the first time and define it.

There can be a power in definitions. Sometimes it is the power to divide up the world. Sometimes it is the power to assign rights. We regularly see this in government legislation and judicial decisions. Instinctively we know that with power comes responsibility, and this is also true of data management. When we create new entity types in data models, or new attributes for these entity types, we are sometimes acting as legislators. No doubt we often collaborate with business users when we do this, but sometimes, especially with metadata, data management acts alone. Acting alone seems to be most frequent with attributes. Suppose some business users decide to create a new attribute called *Customer Lifetime Value* on the entity type **Customer**, and this concept is entirely new to the enterprise. Business users and data management must collaborate to determine how this attribute will be defined. Most likely it will be calculated in some way, but exactly how? This is a creative process more than an analytical one. Idiosyncrasies in pre-existing data may influence the way in which the calculation is done, and they must be entered into the definition.

An example of a metadata attribute might be *Source System Identifier*. This is a field typically placed on all records in an integration hub. It serves to identify the source system from which the record originated. It has (or should have) no meaning to business users. But just what is a source system? Is it the system where the record is originally produced, or a system that directly feeds the integration hub but gets its data from a more upstream system? This information must be placed in a definition.

The responsibility that comes with legislative definitions is that those who create them must use them consistently. In data management there is an unfortunate history of definitions starting off one way for data objects that get implemented in quite another. This is the curse of documentation, which costs a lot to produce but is often distrusted and unused. When it comes to legislative definitions, there simply cannot be any excuse for data management not to keep the definition and the implementation in line. Also the terms used for the concept in question must be used consistently.

10. Indefinables and Near Indefinables

Traditional logicians held that certain things are indefinable. For instance, the classes at the top of logical hierarchies could not be defined because they are not part of anything else. Aristotle identified ten of these supreme genera which he called the "categories" and medieval logicians called the "predicaments." They are: substance, quantity, quality, relation, place, time, position, state, action, and passion. It is not possible to discuss these concepts further here, but the idea that such "ultimates" exist has been a strong influence on logic.

According to philosophers, there are often more synonyms for indefinables than there are for concepts that can be defined. Although data management is not philosophy, it is not uncommon to come across concepts that might not be quite indefinable but are nearly so. All data managers are aware of hierarchies. For instance, going from bottom to top we might have part-time employee – employee – service provider – individual – party. "Party," at the top of this hierarchy, is simply an individual or organization that the enterprise is interested in. There is nothing more to it than that. Similarly "Financial Instrument" may be nothing more than any asset that the enterprise is prepared to trade. In my experience, data managers feel deeply unsatisfied about such definitions. They seem to feel that there must be more objective aspects of "Party" or "Financial Instrument" – something they have missed. Perhaps it is because our education for tests such as the SAT gives us the unquestioned presupposition that every word has a nominal definition. It is time that data managers liberated themselves from such presuppositions and recognized that at the highest levels of abstraction concepts will probably have rather little content in their definitions.

Types of Definition in Information Management

The different types of definition that we have reviewed in this chapter are not all mutually exclusive. Rather they should be seen as different approaches that can be taken to creating and improving definitions. In my experience, data analysts and business analysts receive no guidance on how to formulate definitions and are simply expected to produce them. No template or common pattern is suggested, and definitions vary widely depending on the analyst who is creating them. The different types of definitions at least provide a framework for approaching definition-related tasks. An enterprise can choose which approaches to definitions to follow and which to reject. A priority of types of definition can be set. Definitions can be judged according to which types of definition they incorporate. The trade-offs between the different kinds of definition can be understood over time. Perhaps the biggest error would be to think that there is only one type of definition. This view ignores the fact that we usually come to know a concept gradually, rather than all at once, and that some concepts are initially more difficult to understand than others. Definition is as much process as product. When presented with a series of types we are often tempted to think that one is superior to the others, but this may not really be true of definitions. Finally, the use of types of definition should to some extent be dictated by the goals, culture, resources, and legacy of the enterprise, rather than by purely theoretical considerations.

In examining the various types of real definition, an enterprise should bear in mind the intended uses of the definitions. There may be a trade-off between a type of definition and its intended use. Such trade-offs always occur in design situations, and it should not be expected that a single approach to definitions, excluding all other approaches, will serve all possible needs of an enterprise. For instance, if an enterprise demands that definitions primarily serve to quickly classify instances with concepts, then definitions will focus on providing clearly distinguishing characteristics for each concept. But if an enterprise demands that a definition should fully show how a concept behaves, then distinguishing marks will be of little relevance, and rules describing the behavior of the concept will be of more importance.

Given this, it is wise for any enterprise to consider a strategic approach to definition management in which the trade-offs among the various types of definition can be decided in advance. Or perhaps an approach that utilizes combinations of the different types may be adopted. This latter approach may make definitions longer, but it might satisfy more uses. Each enterprise must make these judgments for itself.

Producing High-Quality Definitions

Eight

Whatever the theoretical basis of definitions, data management requires a practical approach to them. If an enterprise recognizes the value of definitions for data, the next logical step is to determine what is required to create and manage high-quality definitions.

The following is a checklist of criteria by which a definition can be judged to determine if it is well formed.

A Definition Should Be Real, Not Nominal

We explored the distinction between real and nominal definitions in the Chapter 6. A real definition fully explains the nature of something, while a nominal definition explains what a word or term means (its connotation). Much of the literature on definitions states that nominal definitions should be avoided, and real definitions should be preferred.

Perhaps it is true that a nominal definition is minimally useful, but nevertheless it may be a good starting point. Given the difficulty an enterprise may experience in getting to a real definition quickly, a nominal definition may be acceptable at an initial stage, and may be recognized as such. Once again, this procedure suggests that definitions are to be improved over time. Definition is as much process as product.

Perhaps a bigger problem with nominal definitions is that they are what most people think of and experience as definitions. We may assume that definitions should resemble what we find in a dictionary, rather than fully descriptive, real definitions. A typical fallacy, for instance, is that a definition should comprise no more than a single sentence. If this were true, it would make the whole topic of definitions trivial. A definition must be a rather unimportant thing if it can always be expressed in one sentence and anything longer is presumed to be redundancy or loquaciousness. The only reason it seems that dictionaries follow this rule is to reduce space and therefore printing costs. For them it is a economic trade-off, and not adherence to a fundamental property of good definitions. That said, it does seem odd that online-only dictionaries, such as WordNet, still maintain nominal definitions that are highly abbreviated.

Data management must address all false perceptions in an enterprise that come from uncritical familiarity with nominal definitions. Unless this is done, it is unlikely that real definitions will be extensively developed.

A Definition Should Be Complete

This is more of a goal than a qualification for a definition. It is not possible to expect that all definitions will be complete at the outset. We come to know something initially and then gradually get to know it better. Thus, we should expect that all definitions will be improved over time. The expectation that the first version of a definition will be complete is therefore unrealistic.

On the other hand we need a certain level of completeness. A definition that has a significant part omitted is technically termed "elliptical." Elliptical definitions have limited, and sometimes no, use. They can be confusing, and data management cannot afford to be a source of confusion for the enterprise.

A good way to deal with the issue of completeness is to develop a business process that controls the development and publication of definitions, and such processes are discussed more in Chapter 15. The minimum objective is that when a definition is published to the enterprise, it is good enough to be used and will not cause problems. When a definition has reached this level is a matter for judgment. One quick method of reckoning is that, technically speaking, the *definiens* should always be able to substitute for the *definiendum* in cases where the latter is properly used. That is, wherever the term that signifies the concept is used, the statement of the definition can be substituted with no loss or change in meaning.

One danger is that a person may enter an incomplete definition and expect others to complete it, but perhaps no one else will take the time to contribute. A properly designed business process will ensure that incomplete definitions are not left permanently in an incomplete state, by ensuring that individuals are assigned to prevent such problems.

An Entity Instance Cannot Have a Definition, but a Concept Must

Definitions apply to concepts, not individual things. Therefore, individual instances of things cannot be assigned definitions.

Unfortunately, in the world of data management there is often confusion between what an instance is and what a concept is.

For example, suppose we have a reference data code table for Transaction Status Type, with records for

- Ordered
- Paid for
- Shipped
- Received

Some IT professionals believe that because these are four individual records they must represent four individual instances of something. In other words, a record always represents an instance, and an instance never has a definition, and thus a record can never have a definition.

In reality, these four "things" in our example are a breakdown of the generic concept "Transaction Status Type" into four specific concepts. What we have is four instances of concepts. Each record in our table does indeed represent an instance – but it is an instance of a concept. And they are still concepts, even though they are instances of them. Admittedly, this may be rather confusing. However, if something is a concept, then no matter that it is represented in an instance of data, it is still a concept. It still requires a definition. A record that represents a concept is really only an instance from the perspective of data storage and organization, and only an instance of a record type.

Once again the dual nature of data – what it represents versus the data itself – is a source of difficulty. The situation in data management where concepts can be concepts from one perspective and instances from another has no parallel in material reality where types of things do not overlap in this way.

The practical implication for data management is that, unless the concepts that end up as records are assigned definitions, a vast swathe of the data landscape of an enterprise will lack adequate knowledge management. The terms by which these concepts are known, such as "Shipped" in the above example, will be referenced in many places, but will lack any precise definition.

A Definition Must Apply To the Term

A definition can be well formed, but may apply to a concept that is not understood to be signified by the term, and thus be wrong. Dr. Samuel Johnson made some mistakes like this in *A Dictionary of the English Language*, and his biographer, James Boswell, recorded an incident where he was called to task for one:

> "A lady once asked him how he came to define 'pastern', the *knee* of a horse: instead of making an elaborate defence, as might be expected, he at once answered, "Ignorance, Madam, pure ignorance."

The pastern is actually the part of the horse's leg between the fetlock and the hoof.

The chance of making an error in a definition will always be high in an enterprise where specialized jargon prevails, and where definitions are written down by data or business analysts who work for the IT department. Such analysts may never have worked outside an IT department in their entire careers. They cannot be expected to have as deep an understanding of the business of the enterprise as users who spend every day dealing with that business.

This risk must be mitigated, and again, a good way to do so is to have processes for definition management that ensure that knowledgeable individuals examine definitions and ensure they really do define the concept they are supposed to define, and not something else. Periodic re–evaluations and feedback from the media in which the definitions are distributed can also help.

A Definition Must Be Able to Disambiguate an Equivocal Term

A term is said to be *equivocal* when it can mean two or more things, and thus corresponds to two or more concepts. The task of data management is to ensure that each of these concepts has one definition that is not equivocal, and thus must correspond to only one sense in which the term is used. In other words, we must be able to take an equivocal term and resolve it into the homonyms that it covers, and assign the homonyms to distinct concepts. A user must be able to use a definition to clearly understand one specific way in which such a term is used.

This is one of the reasons why a definition should contain something about what the concept it is defining is not. It will help to more clearly distinguish the concept from another concept with which it may be confused, which may be signified by a homonym. Indeed, saying what a concept is not is often necessary, even though this approach is sometimes discouraged in the rather thin literature about practical aspects of definitions. There is general agreement that definitions cannot consist only of describing what something is not. However, this precept cannot be taken so far that it excludes any idea of what is outside the concept referenced in a definition. For example, a definition of a "residential mortgage" might mention that it is not intended for business premises.

A Definition Should Attempt to Cover a Concept

Ideally, a definition should include everything that is intended to be included the concept being defined. Nothing should remain that is not covered by the definition.

If a "residue" remains that would seem to be part of the concept but is not covered by the definition, then we have a problem. This is a key test for a definition. If someone can think of exceptions that should be covered by the definition but are clearly not covered, then the definition is inadequate and may confuse people.

For example, can a commercial real estate mortgage cover a situation where someone owns a variety store but rents out the upper story as apartments? The variety store is commercial real estate, but the rental units are residential. Perhaps the definition of a commercial real estate is intended to exclude this kind of situation. Or perhaps the framers of such a definition simply did not think about such circumstances, and it is a residue.

Unfortunately the world is not as regular and ordered as we like, and so sometimes we are confronted with difficult decisions about definitions. Biologists are familiar with such problems. Mammals usually give live birth to their young, but the duck-billed platypus, classified as a monotreme mammal, lays eggs. On the other hand, the duck-billed platypus has hair and suckles its young – two key characteristics of mammals. Biologists have therefore concluded that if the duck-billed platypus is anything, it is a mammal, and they have classified it accordingly. There will always be difficult cases like this, and some decisions about where to draw the boundaries in a definition will tend to be arbitrary.

One approach is to list the difficult cases in the definition itself. This will provide the reader with a better level of understanding than ignoring such cases would do. People are far more likely to make negative judgments about knowledge-management if they believe that they know significantly more about something than they are being told. The prestige of a set of definitions is likely to be impaired by failure to address difficult cases, and once a negative attitude sets in, it is very difficult to reverse.

Besides difficult cases, modern enterprises must confront evolution in business, legislation, regulation, and so on. These events mean that a sound definition today may not be a sound definition tomorrow. For instance, the Standard Industrial Classification scheme (SIC) was established in the 1930s to classify types of activity in the US economy. The US economy changed more rapidly than the SIC could keep pace with, and the last major revision occurred in 1987. As might be expected, therefore, the SIC classification does not contain anything about the Internet, which is now a major part of the economy.

These kinds of changes happen faster in the aggregate than is generally appreciated. Any particular concept is likely to evolve slowly. However, enterprises deal with so many concepts that there is usually something happening at any one time that could pose a challenge to definitions.

While we need to be comprehensive when developing definitions, there is always a danger of bringing in irrelevant detail. Irrelevant detail can clutter a definition and make it difficult to understand. A user will find it difficult, or perhaps impossible, to understand that an irrelevant point is actually irrelevant. The user may assume it is very important, and confusion will result. Making sure that definitions are properly reviewed can filter out irrelevant points.

A Definition Cannot Exceed the Concept it is Trying to Define

A definition cannot be so broad that it can apply to individual things that lie outside of the concept it defines. Very general definitions are much easier to construct than accurate ones, but they are also confusing. They do not show the boundaries of the concept in question, and it will be difficult to decide which instances are included and which are excluded.

The tendency to general definitions can arise because analysts may be dealing with a term that covers a mixture of concepts – a collection. For instance, let us contrast the definition for "equity" (which can be defined fairly precisely) with that for "financial instrument" (which is much more general). The US Securities and Exchanges Commission (SEC) defines "equity" as follows:

> any stock or similar security, certificate of interest or participation in any profit sharing agreement, preorganization

certificate or subscription, transferable share, voting trust certificate or certificate of deposit for an equity security, limited partnership interest, interest in a joint venture, or certificate of interest in a business trust; any security future on any such security; or any security convertible, with or without consideration into such a security, or carrying any warrant or right to subscribe to or purchase such a security; or any such warrant or right; or any put, call, straddle, or other option or privilege of buying such a security from or selling such a security to another without being bound to do so. [http://www.sec.gov/rules/final/33–8091.htm]

The SEC does not define "financial instrument." Professor Campbell Harvey's Hypertextual Finance Glossary defines "instruments" as

Financial securities, such as money market instruments or capital market instruments. [http://www.duke.edu/~charvey/Classes/wpg/bfglosi.htm]

Professor Harvey's glossary is one of the best in finance, but "financial instrument" is a very vague concept, if indeed it is a concept. In my experience "financial instrument" is the set of types of asset that a particular enterprise trades. For one company it may be only bonds. For another company "financial instrument" may comprise a wide array of assets, perhaps even including gold coins. Such a concept really has validity only within an enterprise, and can be defined only in a very general way if it is to apply to all enterprises. This example illustrates the limits we may encounter when we try to source definitions from outside the enterprise.

Additionally, while it is easy to advise IT personnel that a definition should not exceed the concept it is trying to define, that goal can be very difficult to attain in practice.

A final point here is that brevity in definitions usually leads to loss of detail, and loss of detail can lead to definitions exceeding the concept they are supposed to cover. As has been pointed out before, brevity is typical of nominal definitions in dictionaries, and it must always raise suspicion of the adequacy of a definition.

A Definition Must Not Be Unnecessarily Obscure

A definition cannot be so obscure that it is not easily understood by an individual with reasonable knowledge of the context in which the concept being defined occurs. One of the most famous examples of an obscure definition is Dr. Samuel Johnson's definition for "network":

> any thing reticulated or decussated, at equal distances, with interstices between the intersections

An obscure definition is a risk for confusion. While some kind of definition is nearly always better than no definition at all, if a definition causes problems in the usage of data, such as faulty decision-making, it is not better than no definition at all. There is always a propensity to make definitions obscure in very technical areas, but technical terms are precisely the ones where clear definitions are the most valuable.

As a general rule for definitions, it is often stated that the terms in a definition must all be simpler than the term defined. This objective may be difficult to achieve in practice. After all, technical language may sometimes be needed to properly define a concept. It is also true that some concepts are quite complex, and their definitions will never be immediately understandable to all users. However, it is also possible to have a scale of descriptive meanings within a single definition, such that a beginner can grasp what the definition means, as well as a more precise level on the scale that a technical user can apply.

This raises the fundamental question of the audience that definitions are intended for. In data management, the audience will very likely be knowledge workers within the enterprise. Some level of background understanding must be assumed for this audience. After all, nobody in data management will be writing definitions for, say, kindergarten children. Thus the level of technical language used in definitions must be appropriate. Analysts creating definitions should always ask themselves if every technical term used in the definition is understood by most of the intended audience.

A definition may not always seem obscure to the person or persons creating it. A review process and the solicitation of feedback can assist in identifying obscure definitions. A further process can then be defined in an attempt to clarify any obscure definitions so identified.

A Definition Must Not Contain Further Definitions

A definition must not define other concepts within itself. It may need to refer to other definitions, but these cannot be located within the definition itself.

When this rule is violated, the included definitions are often of poor quality. They cannot be properly managed or governed, they lack supporting metadata, and they are difficult for anyone other than the definers to discover. Where the same concept is defined independently in many locations, it is almost certain that the various definitions will be incompatible – or even contradictory. When many definitions for a given term are distributed over many locations, they will be very difficult to manage. Since there are always many definitions and few data management staff, every effort should be made to reduce the level of management tasks required for definitions in general.

However, controlled redundancy is a different matter. It is possible to have a definition that includes other definitions if the latter are copied in automatically, and reliably, from a single point where they are maintained. It is the maintenance of other definitions within a given definition that is to be avoided.

Design strategies such as hypertext and showing definitions in popup windows greatly diminish the need for included definitions.

Even so, there will always be a tendency to include additional definitions within a definition, and this tendency must be guarded against. Good governance processes can assist in this area.

A Definition Must Not Be Tautological

It is possible to create definitions in which the thing being identified is referred to using another term. These are tautological definitions, and have a structure like the equation A = A. For example, the definition of *human* would be tautological if it were

a member of the species Homo sapiens.

Such a definition provides no information at all. One way to prevent this is not to allow the term being defined to appear in the definition. Technically speaking, we can say that the *definiendum* must not appear in the *definiens*.

This is one of the most common errors in definitions when definitions are formulated by data management personnel, and examples of it can be found in many data models.

Treat Synonyms Correctly

Tautological definitions often involve the use of synonyms. The advice that is often given is to avoid the use of synonyms. However, that would seem to exclude a certain amount of knowledge from the definition. Dealing with synonyms is a different matter from avoiding tautological definitions. There is nothing wrong with a list of synonyms as part of a definition. However, this list should not be the basis by which the concept being defined is made understandable.

Not only should synonyms be avoided in a definition, but so should near-synonyms. For example, "database" cannot be defined using a synonym, such as "data repository," or a near synonym, such as "data store."

However, in nominal definitions, synonyms are commonly used, and they easily achieve the brevity usually required of nominal definitions. This technique appears to be more successful when the concept involved is widely shared.

With definitions in data management, there will always be a portion of the definition that applies to the thing represented and another that applies to the data-centric aspects of the representation. It is reasonable to assume that for commonly understood concepts a nominal definition suffices for the thing represented, whereas much more of a real definition is needed for the way it is represented in data. Obviously, this requires judgment and discipline, and analysts should not take it as an excuse to fall back into the abbreviated phrases so common in the nominal definitions of dictionaries, and which so often simply employ synonyms.

A Definition Must Not Be Circular

It is possible to have circular references among definitions, where one is built upon a second, but the second is built upon the first. Consider the definition for "day":

a period of 24 hours

Now consider the definition for "hour":

one twenty–fourth part of a day

Each of these definitions references the other and is understandable only in terms of the other – which refers directly back to the one we started with. We have a closed loop, and hence they are called "circular definitions." These types of definitions can be extremely frustrating to users.

In the special case of relative terms that are needed to define each other, the related term may appear in the definition of the other term – for example, "later" and "earlier, where "earlier" is defined as:

a point in time prior to a later point in time.

Thus, there may be some situations in which a degree of circularity is unavoidable.

The problem of circular definitions is not easy to manage in an environment where many individuals contribute to definitions. One way to deal with it is to have an automated search of definitions to discover what terms occur in each definition, and whether these terms have definitions that include the original term. For instance, in the example given above, the definition for "day" would be found to include the term "hour" and the definition for "hour" would be found to include the term "day." A report of such cases could then be used to manually examine the definitions involved to determine if circularity existed.

A Definition Should Not Be Negative if it Can Be Positive

It is always better to define something by what it is rather than what it is not. However, as noted above, it is also good to add further information to a positive definition about what the concept is not. This helps to increase the understanding of the scope and boundaries of the concept.

One way to deal with this is to have the positive aspects appear first in a definition. They can then be followed by the negative aspects.

However, some terms are inherently negative, such as

"overdraft," "default," "foreclosure," "bankruptcy." Thus it is not always possible to avoid using a negative definition. For example, "Referential Integrity Error" could be defined as follows:

Occurs only in a child column that is a migrated foreign key from a parent table. It happens when a value found in the child column does not occur in the set of data values found in the corresponding parent column.

In such cases, definitions must have a negative cast. Even so, this is still a little different from saying what something is not, and even a definition with a negative cast may still need to include additional statements about what it is not. For instance, a default may be defined as

payments not received for 90 days.

Yet it may be necessary to add to this definition that an account in default is one that has not yet been handed over to a collection agency. Again, saying what it is not helps to draw the boundaries even of a concept that is basically negative.

Make Ambiguity Explicit

Ambiguity arises when the meaning of something cannot be determined. It is hardly surprising that definitions may involve ambiguity. Perhaps we come across a new, unfamiliar concept, or perhaps a new piece of business jargon can be applied in different ways.

There is a tendency in analysis to record only what is unambiguously known. However, analysis is not journalism. If we know that we do not know something, then that lack of knowledge should be placed in the text of a definition, even if it is only temporary and the ambiguity is resolved later. Not knowing potential pitfalls is hardly helpful to a user of a definition.

A Definition Should Not Be an Enumeration of Instances

A list of all, or many, of the instances known to be covered by a concept is not a definition. It will never tell us why these instances are thought to be covered by the concept, or what they have in common.

When a list of instances is provided as a definition, there is often reason to believe that we are dealing with a collection of concepts that the enterprise has grouped together for some reason, and that there is nothing objective in common among these concepts apart from the enterprise's intentions for them.

In the case of collections, the definition may therefore have to consist of the enterprise's intentions for the collection, rather than an effort to look outside of the context of the enterprise to find some commonality among the diverse set of concepts that make it up. Such commonality may not exist.

Of course, it is an excellent practice to include examples in a definition. Such examples help the readers to validate their understanding of the definition. A reader can perhaps understand why some instances are present. Perhaps the reader may not immediately grasp why other instances are included as examples. This may make readers realize that they have not fully understood the definition, and hopefully will spur them to reflect on it more.

A Definition Must Not Be Self-Contradictory

This seems like a fairly obvious piece of advice, but sometimes definitions may be unintentionally self-contradictory. For example, "Optional Task" may be defined as

a task the operating system allocates to a server to run.

The task is hardly optional from the server's perspective.

Self-contradiction should be caught in the review of definitions, which should be part of the processes implemented to govern definitions. Also, permitting feedback on definitions can lead to identifying self-contradiction.

Avoid Using Definitions to Persuade

Being impartial is not always an easy task, but we must strive to maintain it. Definitions have often been seen as an area by which unscrupulous individuals push hidden agendas. It is not difficult to see how they can use definitions to do this. If a definition can be crafted that implies a particular perspective or course of action, and that definition is then promoted, the definition gives the appearance of a sound logical ground supporting the viewpoint of the definer. For instance, Karl Marx defined "capital" (or at least produced a description very close to a definition) this way:

> Capital is dead labor, which, vampire-like, lives only by sucking living labor, and lives the more, the more labor it sucks." [*Das Kapital*, Volume 1, Chapter 10]

Even in the humble domain of data management, it is possible to produce definitions that are aligned with particular political interests in the enterprise. Perhaps data in one particular database could have definitions suggesting that it is of poor quality, while definitions for a rival database could have definitions that suggest it has better quality than it in fact does. Most data managers with sufficient experience will recognize such situations.

These temptations introduce irrelevant detail into the definitions, and ultimately detract from their usefulness. Definitions should be used to inform, not persuade.

Avoid Using Emotive Language

Very similar to hijacking definitions for the purposes of persuasion, is the use of expressive or emotional language when constructing them. Indeed, emotive definitions often overlap with persuasive ones. All emotive and expressive language should be excluded from definitions. Unfortunately, even the greatest minds can succumb to the temptation. For instance, Dr. Johnson once defined "oats" as

A grain, which in England is generally given to horses, but in Scotland appears to support the people.

Dr. Johnson took occasional verbal shots at the Scots, and this is one of his more famous ones. There is really no excuse for this kind of performance by anyone producing definitions today.

There is no reason to believe that data management is immune to this problem. Impartiality requires effort, and data managers must have the discipline to focus only on the best possible definition.

Manage Repetition, Redundancy, and Explanation

There is often a general dislike of repetition and redundancy in any documentation, and it is fair to say that simple repetition is hardly ever justified.

However, some degree of redundancy may be necessary in definitions. If an idea is stated only once, then the reader has just one chance to grasp it. However, if an idea is stated in a few different ways then the reader has a greater chance of understanding it. We have probably all had the experience of admiring a very well-written text that contains a passage we could not understand. If the author had written the passage differently, then perhaps we could have understood it, but another reader might not have. Casting the information to be conveyed from more than one perspective can help to reduce this problem. Also, a given point may be significant in more than one way, and each of these kinds of significance may need to be brought out.

To some degree, redundancy is more a technique of explanation than of definition. Explanation is the means of bringing the mind to understand something, and is a different area from definition. The boundary between explanation and definition may be difficult to find, and there is a danger that definitions may try to become explanations. If this happens, the definition may start to expand to cover more than one concept and not provide its intended audience with the information it needs. Most definitions must assume a certain degree of pre-existing knowledge in order to contain their scope. However, this is a very difficult area and will depend to some extent on who the definitions are written for. If definitions start to become explanations, then this may be a sign that a training manual or similar document needs to be developed.

Attention to Audience

As noted above in the discussion of obscure definitions, it is important to understand the intended audience. There are three potential groups involved in definitions:

- the individuals who create the definitions

- the individuals who will use the definitions

- the individuals who deal with the concepts and terms that the definitions cover

There is a tendency in data management not to understand or profile the communities for whom artifacts of analysis are intended. The most dangerous result of such neglect is to create definitions that are really intended only for those that create them. There is nothing inherently wrong with the creators being the users of the definitions, but when they are the only users, the definitions tend to be of poor quality because there is no expectation of external criticism.

If work done on data definitions is to be valuable, it must cover as much of each of the three groups identified above as possible. This will provide the greatest potential payback for the resources the enterprise invests in the creation of the definitions. A "build it and they will come" attitude will not guarantee this, which is why some degree of market analysis of the potential target audiences is necessary. This is not a traditional activity in IT, and is more art than science. Yet, as data management matures, it will require more of these "softer" skills if it is to succeed.

Conclusion

The checklist presented above does not exhaust all the possibilities involved in producing high-quality definitions, but it is a starting point. A couple of sample definitions based on this checklist and other considerations discussed in the following chapters are presented in *Appendix 5*.

Every enterprise that strives to produce high-quality definitions should have some documentation on the criteria for achieving them. It could be very helpful to develop a training program that includes material on such criteria. Above all, a practical approach must always be taken. There are dangers in taking any of the criteria discussed here to extremes. Judgment is called for, and that judgment must always reflect on the usage and value of definitions to the enterprise.

Nine

Nine

Nine

Entity Type Versus Attribute Definitions

So far we have looked at definitions mostly from the perspective of the traditional approaches that may apply to data management. Now we will begin to look more closely at the specific requirements of data management. First, we need to deal with the possibility that in data management some things can be defined simply by aggregating definitions of other things that compose them.

As we saw earlier, there are many different kinds of metadata and data objects. However, some of these entities appear to be logical divisions of others. In particular, attributes appear to be "children" of entity types, and columns "children" of tables. One entity type will nearly always have many attributes, and one table will nearly always have many columns. From the point of view of definitions, the question arises as to whether, once we have defined all the attributes, we need a definition of the "parent" entity type, and, similarly, if we define all the columns is there any need to have a definition of the "parent" table?

This problem can be stated in a slightly different way. Data modeling leads to the identification and design of entity types. Each entity type in a logical data model is supposed to be fully attributed. That is, all the attributes that the enterprise must manage for the entity type are added to the data model. Eventually, at least in theory, the entity types are implemented as tables in a database, and the attributes are implemented as columns within the respective tables. Why, then, worry about definitions for entity types and tables? If we have the lists (and definitions) of the attributes and columns, is that all that is needed?

Distinctive Definitions

This problem applies particularly to distinctive definitions. As we saw in the chapter on types of definition, distinctive definitions consist of the characteristics of the things being defined. In logical data modeling, characteristics become attributes of entity types, and definitions are supplied for them.

It is evidently a mistake, therefore, to (a) list attributes and define them within the definition of the entity type, and to then (b) separately identify all the attributes and give each one a definition. This practice can be quite confusing. Everyone would agree that attribute definitions belong with the attributes they are defining, not the entity type to which the attributes belong. But if we take this approach, what will be left over for a definition of an entity type?

One answer is that not all characteristics of an entity type may be captured in the attributes of a data model. If characteristics are not captured as attributes, then the only place that remains where they can be described is the definition of the entity type. For instance, suppose we are defining the entity type **Customer** and no customer can be under 18 years of age. Age is definitely an attribute of **Customer,** but it is very unlikely we will store it, because it must be recalculated every day. Instead we will probably have an attribute *Customer Date of Birth*. Then, in the definition of **Customer** we can state something like

> *Every customer must be 18 years of age or over. Age is calculated as the date of any transaction with a potential customer, minus Customer Date of Birth.*

In this way we can add to the distinctive definition of **Customer** without having to declare an attribute whose values would be troublesome to maintain.

A second issue is that certain attributes may have specific relationships. This is a very troubling area in data management because it is difficult to reconcile with pure relational theory. Be that as it may, it happens very often. For instance, suppose we have an entity type **Financial Instrument** that has the attributes *Financial Instrument Type Code* and *Maturity Date*. We may have a rule that if a record has *Financial Instrument Type Code* = "BOND," then *Maturity Date* must have a valid value, but for every other value of *Financial Instrument Type Code*, the value of *Maturity Date* must be null. If we put this information into the definition of the attribute *Financial Instrument Type Code*, then someone looking at the definition of *Maturity Date* will not be aware of the rule. If we put this information into the definition of the *Maturity Date*, then someone looking at the definition of *Financial Instrument Type Code* will not be aware of the rule. If we put the rule in both attributes, then we will have to remember to update it in both places if it ever changes, and there is nothing to stop the two pieces of information diverging or conflicting over time. Lastly, nobody will be aware of the rule unless they know that it is contained in one or both of the attribute definitions.

Given this, in the absence of other ways of managing definitions, it will be best to contain this rule in the definition of the entity type **Financial Instrument**. If a user wants to know the definition of **Financial Instrument**, the user will then discover the rule there.

Otherwise, users may not see it, and may not be aware that they must read every attribute definition.

Now, it must be admitted that the problems outlined above can be solved by other designs. For instance, the design could be such that, when a user brings up the definition of an entity type, all the definitions of the attributes of the entity type might be included in the display. Alternatively, there may be a commitment to managing business rules separate to entities and attributes. In that case, the information about the interaction of *Financial Instrument Type Code* and *Maturity Date* may be placed in structured metadata for business rules that is located outside of definitions for entity type and attributes. Of course, users must then be trained in how to navigate such an environment.

Nevertheless, we can see from this that we cannot easily eliminate definitions at the entity type and table levels, even if we want only to store distinctive definitions.

Existence

Distinctive definitions may be popular because they are the type most commonly encountered in natural science, but they have some limitations. A particular limitation is that a list of attributes may not tell us much about the existence of instances of the entity type in question.

The problem of existence is not uncommon and can present real headaches in data management. For instance, can a given person legitimately have more than one customer record in an enterprise's databases? Can we add an account record if we do not already have a record for a fully identified customer who owns the account? Should currency be treated as an equity by a financial services company, or is it something else? Are we supposed to report trades over a certain dollar value? These kinds of questions pertain more to the existence or non-existence of records in a table, rather than any characteristics of an existing record.

Existence is one of the areas in data management where questions arise that are often difficult to answer, and perhaps even difficult to articulate. Suppose a user comes across an account record that does not appear to be for any customer. Is this an error, or is there some reason for the account to be there, such as an accounting contrivance? Perhaps it was a quick, one-time solution for reversing an error of several years ago.

Non-existence is another such issue. We may need to exclude certain things from a database table. Suppose we have a **Customer** table that is intended only for residents of the USA and Canada. Perhaps this table will not have a column such as *Customer Country of Residence*, and it is simply expected that the information will be obtained during the customer on-boarding process, and ineligible individuals will not be accepted as customers. It is difficult to see where the rule that only US and Canadian citizens can be customers could be stored other than the table definition.

The Limits of Distinctive Definitions

Distinctive definitions are the norm in natural science, and natural science has been so successful that it often seems to be a model for all other areas of human endeavor. This implies that we should adopt distinctive definitions, and distinctive definitions can indeed be very helpful as part of our knowledge about data. However, we need to recognize that data management is different from studying naturally occurring phenomena and that distinctive definitions based on sets of characteristics may not be sufficient for data and metadata objects that are composed of such sets of characteristics. The whole is not necessarily the sum of the parts, and in any case we may not have all of the parts under management. Beyond this, there are areas that are not really characteristics of something. Purpose, described in the chapter on types of definitions, is one example. Clearly purpose does not fit with distinctive definitions, but it is really vital in data management.

Thinking that an entity type is no more than the sum of its attributes could be a real danger in the area of the semantic web. The semantic web is relatively immature, but if the "semantics" are treated as no more than lists of attributes for an entity type, our ability to attain the goals of the semantic web may be severely limited. That, however, is a different discussion, and one whose outcome must probably wait some years.

Precision of Data

We now move more into purely data-centric consider-ations for definitions in data management. The first such area is precision.

Precision in data is conventionally applied only to quantitative types of data. It can be defined as

the level of detail to which the data is claimed to be reliable.

There are other ways in which "precision" has been used. It can mean a high degree of approximation in any kind of descrip-tion (including definitions). It has been used to mean the ability to focus on a particular element of something we perceive. However, perhaps because of the way in which datatypes have been devel-oped, in the domain of data, precision is concerned with the degree of resolution of quantitative data.

In practice, this means the order of magnitude of whole numbers, or the number of decimal places for values that includes a level of detail that lies between 0 and either 1 or –1.

This is not the same concept as precision in measurement, which can be defined as

the degree to which repeated measurements show the same results under constant conditions.

Measurement is nearly always recorded as data, so there is a strong relationship between measurement and data. However, the concept of precision in measurement cannot apply to a single data point, because by definition some degree of repetition is implied. Nor can it apply to the schema of a field, such as a column definition in a database table.

Precision in data may be artificially decided simply as a reporting convention to permit humans to better appreciate the data being presented. For instance, the US Federal Reserve Bank reported in its Combined Statements of Condition for 2008 the value of its Gold Certificates in *millions of US dollars* (http://www.federalreserve.gov/monetarypolicy/files/BSTFRcombinedfinstmt20072008.pdf). The number reported was

$11,037 (millions of US Dollars).

This number would be fully expressed as

$11,037,000,000 (US Dollars).

The resolution of this data – its precision – is therefore to the nearest million dollars.

In this form the number is easy to appreciate. Perhaps it was rounded up from a more precise number, or perhaps some other explanation applies. In any event, all the numbers on the Combined Statements of Condition are in millions of dollars. This approach makes comparing the figures much easier.

However, when numbers are stated in millions, we have no expectation that the data will have a level of precision greater than the next million dollars. If such numbers are expressed as whole numbers, the thousands, hundreds, and tens columns must all be zero.

Now, it is not certain if the numbers in this report were rounded up to the nearest million when they were reported, and if in the underlying database they were stored in a more precise format – say, to the nearest dollar. Precision, however, always deserves consideration for mention in the definition of an attribute, column, or field. This becomes more obvious when we distinguish data content from structure.

Very occasionally a number may not be rounded off, but may give the appearance of being rounded off. For instance, prices in a currency that has suffered hyperinflation maybe quoted in thousands. Once again, though, this fact should be captured in a definition.

Implied Precision Greater than Actual Precision

Data content is one thing, but data structure is another. Data structure includes datatypes, which specify the orders of magnitude and numbers of decimal places that can be stored in a field for quantitative data. Sometimes, however, there is a mismatch between the data content and the datatype

For instance, the Federal Reserve Gold Certificate value could be stored in a field that permitted 8 decimal places. This would make the $11,037 million appear as 11037000000.00000000 if the database were browsed directly. It is natural for anyone using the data to interpret the content of such a field as having the precision implied by the datatype of the field – at least in the absence of any other information on how to interpret the data content. But in the present example, this is not the case because the data content is rounded to the nearest million. The datatype is therefore misleading and may lead to an improper interpretation.

In such cases it is necessary to specify the precision of the data in the definition. In the example given above it would be necessary to state that the precision of the data content is to the nearest million, irrespective of the datatype of the field.

This kind of problem, where actual precision is different from that implied by the datatype, is far from uncommon. It needs to be detected and understood if data is to be used properly, especially if data is to be moved to an integrated environment such as a data warehouse. Unless precision is reliably specified in data definitions, profiling is often needed to reveal the true nature of the data. Such profiling is expensive and consumes time and human resources.

Regrettably, once data profiling reveals the true nature of the precision of data content, this result is rarely stored in a data definition held in a permanent and shared repository. That state of affairs in turn usually means that data profiling must be repeated as time passes and knowledge of the state of precision of the data is gradually lost, or as analysts feel unsure that the results of the previous profiling exercise may still be applicable.

Storing Data at Higher Place Values

Another kind of problem occurs if we choose to store the $11,037,000,000 in the form that it is represented in the Federal Reserve Bank's reporting – that is, as millions. Thus, the number would be stored as a straight integer with the value 11037. It must be "understood" that this content represents *millions of dollars,* and not *single dollars*. But where will this knowledge be stored so that an uninitiated user will not be confused? The following options suggest themselves:

- Perhaps it will not be stored at all, which could only mean that it would become "tribal knowledge," passed around by word of mouth, or figured out independently.

- Perhaps the knowledge might be stored in the field name. It could be called *Federal Gold Certificate Value in Millions of US Dollars*. It is very unlikely that such a name would be implemented for a database column because it is too long.

- Perhaps the knowledge would be implemented by a separate field to store the units in which the value is stored. For example, a field called *Federal Gold Certificate Value Units*. This would have a value of 1,000,000 in every instance, which seems rather redundant and unnecessary. It would also be necessary to know that this second field is related to the original field containing the Federal Gold Certificate Value. This increases the amount of knowledge to be managed and adds to the overall burden of work.

None of these three alternatives is very good. The better alternative is to maintain all knowledge of how to interpret the data content of the field in the definition. If the definition is known to be less than the total knowledge needed to describe what the data means, and what it represents, then nobody will fully trust the definition to provide this information, and users must search for it elsewhere.

Of course, it is always possible to avoid this problem by consistently storing integer data in units. Thus, in the current example, that would mean storing the data value as 11037000000. Data standards like this can be very useful. However, the problem of implied precision being greater than actual precision remains, and so the need to manage some amount of knowledge is unavoidable.

Derived Data and Precision

Suppose we decided that we would like to calculate the equivalent of the value of the US Federal Reserve Bank's 2008 Gold Certificates in units of pure gold. Let us call this new field *Gold Certificates Metal Equivalent*. It seems fairly obvious that we can do this by dividing the reported Gold Certificate value by the current price of an ounce of gold. If the current price of gold is $1040.40 then we calculate

Gold Certificates Metal Equivalent = 11,037,000,000 / 1,040.40 = 10,608,419.83 ounces.

We have chosen, quite arbitrarily, to store this data to two decimal places. But how justified are we in doing this? Suppose that the original 11,037,000,000 was rounded to the nearest million. If this were so, then the 11,037,000,000 would really be plus or minus 1,000,000. This lack of precision will be inherited by the *Gold Certificates Metal Equivalent*. The calculation could therefore be wrong by (plus or minus)

(1,000,000 / 1,040.40) / 2 = 480.585 ounces.

A major problem is that, because we have decided to calculate and store this data to two decimal places, we cannot discover by data profiling the fact that there is a tolerance of plus or minus 480.585 ounces. In the case of the data about the Gold Certificates themselves, profiling would, of course, reveal that all figures had no resolution below one million dollars.

Now, this kind of problem leads very quickly into the area of statistical management, which is quite different from managing data definitions, and well beyond the scope of this book. Nevertheless, data managers should be careful when dealing with derived and computed data to ensure that there is a complete understanding of the characteristics of precision inherited in the derived data element from source data elements.

Rounding

Rounding is a topic that is closely related to precision. It may seem arcane and rather boring, but in the aggregation of derived numbers in environments such as data warehouses it can cause enormous headaches.

Rounding becomes an issue when the result of a calculation has non-zero numbers in decimal places beyond the number of decimal places allowed by the datatype of the field in which the result will be stored.

Consider this calculation:

2.25 x 3.15 = 7.0875.

Suppose the result can be stored only in a field that permits two decimal places. What should be done with the part of the number beyond two decimal places? A common approach would be to add a value of 5 at the next decimal place beyond that included in the datatype and truncate the result. For the above example,

7.0875 + 0.005 = 7.0925.

7.0925 truncated to two decimal places = 7.09.

Thus we would store the value 7.09. What we have just done is to apply a rounding rule. There are a number of different rules that can be used to do rounding, and in a given enterprise there is often no guarantee that a single standard rule will be used. In fact there may be reasons to use different rules in different circumstances.

The best course, therefore, is to store the rounding rule in the field definition.

Unfortunately, it does not stop here. If we go back to our example, there is a difference between the calculated result and the stored result:

7.09 (stored result) − 7.0825 (calculated) = 0.0075.

This may seem like a small difference, but when millions of calculations are performed and fed into chains of millions of more calculations, the differences that are lost can aggregate to significant values. One solution may be to keep the rounding differences in memory as a set of calculations are performed and ultimately store the aggregated rounding errors in a separate field. The existence and meaning of this field should be referenced in the definition of the field in which the rounded result is stored. Of course, this is an area where programming techniques, database design, and statistical concerns must be addressed, but nevertheless the implications for definitions must not be overlooked.

Eleven

Accuracy
of
Data

ccuracy is
the degree to which data really represents what
it is intended to represent.

It is sometimes confused with precision, which we considered
in the previous chapter. For instance, I can guess that there is a
17.125 percent chance of snow 25 days from now. My guess is
precise – to three decimal places. However, I can guarantee that
it is wildly inaccurate and bears no resemblance to the reality of
what the weather will be in 25 days time. Unfortunately, a very
precise number sometimes fools us into thinking that it must be
accurate just because it is precise. This is not so, because accuracy
is not the same as precision.

Accuracy and Measurement

Accuracy, like precision, is a term used to signify a concept in
measurement. It is the degree to which a measurement actually

matches the real value measured. However, it should be remembered that measurement is (or should be) a relative process. It is the comparison of a characteristic of a real object to a reference standard. This complex of at least (a) the thing being measured, (b) the measurement apparatus and methodology, and (c) the reference standard is not the same as data. When data represents measurements, this concept of accuracy may be applicable.

For instance, I can use a ruler to measure the width of a sheet of paper, and find it is 21 cm. The centimeter is the reference standard here. It is one hundredth of a meter. A meter was originally specified as one ten–millionth of the distance from the equator to the North Pole. Later the standard changed to the length of a rod of platinum kept in Paris, and later still it became a certain number of wavelengths of light of a certain frequency. Measurement always involves the comparison of a quantitative attribute to a reference standard of this type.

In the case of data that represents measurements, we must record the limits of accuracy inherent in the data. But data is not always like the quantitative data that is the norm in scientific work. In most enterprises, qualitative data like names and addresses makes up a considerable portion of the data. The idea of accuracy in measurement does not directly apply to qualitative data, because data like names and addresses is not gathered by measurement.

For definitions, therefore, the role of accuracy needs to be carefully considered, and also the special application of accuracy to quantitative versus qualitative data needs to be understood.

Is Ultimate Accuracy Impossible?

Let us first begin with quantitative measurements and their attributes. W. Edwards Deming (1900–1993) was one of the individuals most responsible for evangelizing and implementing quality control in the USA and Japan. He made the following astonishing statement in his foreword to the 1986 edition of *Statistical Method from the Viewpoint of Quality Control*, written by his mentor, Walter A. Shewhart (1891–1967).

> There is no true value of anything. There is instead a figure that is produced by application of a master or ideal method of counting or measurement.... There is no true value of the speed of light; no true value of the number of inhabitants within the boundaries of (e.g.) Detroit. A count of the number of inhabitants of Detroit is dependent upon the arbitrary rules for carrying out the count. Repetition of an experiment or of a count will exhibit variation. Change in the method of measuring the speed of light produces a new result.

Deming knew what he was talking about. He was involved in the 1940 US Census and the 1951 Japanese Census. In the former he introduced sampling techniques that greatly reduced error rates. Deming was a physicist by training, and much of his quality control work focused on manufacturing.

There can be little doubt that Deming was talking about data produced by measurement, and to him accuracy was a problem in inherent in the measurement process.

Shewhart and Deming distinguished two different areas from which errors in measurement – inaccuracies – could arise. One of these areas was systemic causes. With systemic causes, something specific is wrong in the system and/or methods used to produce the measurements. For instance, sampling voter intentions of a population by using the customer list of Rolls-Royce dealerships will likely skew the sample to very rich people and not be truly representative of voters. The other area Shewhart and Deming saw as a source of error was chance errors – random variations that ultimately limit accuracy. For instance, such errors may occur when I use a ruler to measure the diameter of tomatoes, and both ruler and tomatoes expand or contract with temperature, and temperature fluctuates from time to time when I am making my measurements.

One way to deal with these issues is to describe the methods and equipment used to make the measurements as part of the definitions of the data. Regrettably, this is all too often absent, even in scientific data sets.

Furthermore, it is necessary to know what systemic errors are corrected and when they are corrected. After all, when such an error is corrected, the nature of the data will change.

In many enterprises there are few data elements whose values are based on physical measurement. Where they do exist, it may be worth including descriptions of methods and equipment in the definitions. Some enterprises may indeed be highly concerned about physical measurements, and in these situations structured metadata may be the best choice to hold information about the methods and equipment used. That is, additional data elements can be put into a database to hold information such as the type of equipment used and the environmental conditions, such as the temperature and pressure prevailing when measurements are to be made.

However, this approach is really worthwhile only for factors that vary for individual measurements. If one piece of equipment is used to make measurements for several years, and is eventually replaced by a different piece of equipment, it may be felt unnecessary to create additional fields in the database to hold this information. Instead, placing the information in the definition along with the date of the changeover may be a better option.

Accuracy and Qualitative Attributes

As noted above, much data consists of qualitative attributes – like customer name and address. This kind of data is not obtained by measurement involving some reference standard such as meters or kilograms. Therefore, accuracy for qualitative data is bound to be different from accuracy for quantitative data (or at least the kind of quantitative data based on measurement using a reference standard). It is difficult to see how Deming's statement that "there is no true value of anything" can apply to qualitative data. We can get a name or an address wrong, but we can also capture it with complete accuracy. Admittedly, quantitative attributes can be based on qualitative attributes, but these will tend to be counts and ratios based on counts. Deming's claim may hold true for this kind of data, but it cannot be extended back to the underlying qualitative data.

Many issues can affect the accuracy of qualitative data in many ways. This leads into the area of data quality, which is outside the scope of this book. However, one of the ideas that has come from the data quality discipline may be applicable to definitions: Accuracy can be broken down into a number of categories. These categories may be candidates for inclusion in definitions. Some examples include the following:

- **Timeliness.** A system may be aware of a customer, perhaps via some national identifier, but the customer's name may be provided only at a later date. The average time for the name to become known could be included in a definition.

- **Decay.** Customers will change their address every so often, but some of these changes will go unreported. Thus the longer an address remains unchanged in a database, the higher the chance that it will be wrong. Such a statistic could be expressed as the percentage of unchanged addresses that are assumed to become inaccurate every month. However, the more seriously an enterprise takes such information, the more likely it is that such a piece of information will be moved out of a definition into structured metadata and become a metric that is tracked over time. Perhaps the lesson here is that information about accuracy can be stored in a definition until it is moved into structured metadata.

- **Transcription Errors.** Suppose information is provided on handwritten forms and these are data entered into a system. Mistakes can be made in this transcription process. Perhaps there are illegible entries on the form. Or perhaps the data entry operator might put *Customer Last Name* in the *Customer First Name* field on the screen. "Fat fingering" of the keyboard, such as hitting the "S" key instead of the "A" key is another problem. There are algorithms that can detect – to some extent – these kinds of problem. The ways in which such algorithms are employed could be included in the definition.

This list can go on. There are probably many more categories of data quality errors, and each of them has special features that can be included in the definition of the affected data. The problem is that there is no single theoretical basis for all of them in the same way as there is for the concept of accuracy in measurement. Each must be treated on an individual basis. Here, though, we are again straying from the domain of data definitions into the domain of data quality. Definitions are not the place for all aspects of knowledge about data quality, but in the absence of specialized structured metadata, they may be the only place available to store this information.

Accuracy and Definition

Hopefully, in the future, the role of accuracy in data will be better understood as the theory and practice of data quality are developed. For now, it would seem that several items of information could be stored in data definitions:

- **Process of Data Collection.** A description of how the data being defined is collected, together with known issues about accuracy in the process. Any methodology could be included here too. If measuring instruments are used, they can be described. Instruments often have known tolerances that affect accuracy of measurement.

- **Accuracy Metrics Maintained Elsewhere.** With the growth of metrics used to measure data quality, it is possible that the data being defined will have associated metrics describing its accuracy stored in some other part of the database (or even in a different database). The locations in which these metrics are stored – and links to their definitions – can be referenced in the definition of the data object for which the metrics measure. Similarly, the definition of each metric can refer back to the definition of the data object whose accuracy the metric measures.

- **Known Sources of Inaccuracy.** The definition of a data object can be enhanced by updating it to include every known problem about its accuracy. These problems may or may not be organized according to a categorization of data-quality issues. Events where accuracy is an issue can also be recorded in this way.

- **Accuracy of Interpretation.** Accuracy may not end with the data itself once data values have been populated into a database. Some data may have a propensity to be interpreted or used inaccurately. Knowledge workers can be warned about such dangers in the definition, and can be advised as to how to interpret the data accurately. This aspect of accuracy is often not discussed in the discipline of data quality.

- **Decay Rate of Data.** As mentioned above, data may be accurate at one point in time but not at another. This is truer of things, which can change, than events, which can never change. Events may be recorded inaccurately, and the data for them may need to be changed at a later time, but the basic event happens and never changes thereafter. Things do change, and even the rules that prescribe the behavior of things may change over time. Knowledge workers need to be aware of how accurate the data about them is, relative to their age. This is very difficult to judge, but even anecdotal information may be useful.

This approach to dealing with accuracy is based on the idea that a definition is a central point for recording all information needed to understand a data object, or at least for providing a reference to all such information. Thus, knowledge workers will know that they can find out everything that is known about accuracy for a data object by consulting its definition. The approach can equally be used for qualitative aspects and quantitative aspects of accuracy.

Twelve

Twelve

Scope
of
Data

When we ask of data "What is it?" we are usually trying to understand the definitions of the concepts that the data is intended to represent. When we ask "What does it mean?" we are usually trying to match up terms used to label the data to the concepts we already understand. These two questions – "What is it?" and "What does it mean?" – echo the philosopher and the lexicographer. And if they were all that were really needed to understand data, then the keys to data management would lie in philosophy and lexicography. Alas, issues inherent in data are much more complex than can be solved by assuming that other areas of human endeavor already have the answers. Data has unique characteristics and behaviors. It needs to be understood in its own right, and not as a phenomenon that is wholly explicable from perspectives outside of data itself.

One of the problems inherent in data that prevent us from giving an adequate answer to the questions "What is it?" and "What does it mean?" is that data always has some kind of scope. Take for instance, an **Employee** table in a human resources database. A philosopher would answer the question of what an employee is in a way that would cover the entire concept of "employee" and "employment" in a way that would, presumably, be relevant to every enterprise. The philosopher's work might be quite useful to legislators and lawyers trying to frame and implement labor laws. But nobody would expect such a definition to tell us everything we need to know about the **Employee** table in our particular enterprise. A lexicographer's definition would similarly be of very limited use for understanding the **Employee** table. It would just tell us something about how the word "employee" is used.

So, when we ask "What is it?" and "What does it mean?" about the **Employee** table, we are asking for a far more detailed understanding of the data than the form of the questions we are asking may imply. In fact, it is often frustrating to ask questions about data because we feel that we cannot even frame the questions adequately for the kind of answers we are looking for. This frustration with data is far more common than is generally recognized or admitted, and will be alleviated only as we treat data as an area of human endeavor that must be worked out, as we have worked out other areas.

Scope

Let us make the following suppositions about our Employee table:

- Suppose the **Employee** table contains records for individuals who have a permanent employment contract with the enterprise.

- Suppose the table contains records for short–term contractors who are employed on an individual basis, but not short-term contractors who are employed through a subcontracting company.

- Suppose the table contains records for individuals hired in the United States of America but not individuals hired in Canada. Our enterprise has a completely separate system and database in Canada to deal with the operations there.

- However, suppose that Canadian employees who are seconded to positions in locations in the United States do have records entered for them into the **Employee** table.

- Suppose that employee records are purged from the table 180 days after an employee resigns, or 30 days after an individual subcontractor is not renewed, or 90 days after a seconded Canadian returns to Canada.

None of this information about our **Employee** table is suggested by the questions "What is it?" and "What does it mean?" It is not anything that would occur to a philosopher or lexicographer to include in their definitions. And yet it is definitional information. It clearly delineates the boundaries of the data – at least in our hypothetical enterprise – and shows what is included and excluded. But what exactly are we talking about here?

The answer is that this information describes the scope of the data. What is "scope"? *Baldwin's Dictionary of Philosophy and Psychology* defines it this way:

> The aggregate of subjects to which a term, proposition, reasoning, inquiry, treatise, etc., refers or is intended to refer; the logical breadth. Cf. EXTENSION (in logic).

Now, the term "extension" referred to in this definition is an old one in logic. It represents an important concept that has largely been lost because traditional logic is no longer taught widely in the West. Turning again to Baldwin, we find "extension" defined as follows:

> The extension or extent of a general notion is the whole range of concrete objects, lower classes, cases, or instances

in which are found the distinctive characters making up the comprehension of the said notion....

The distinction between the two aspects of all generalizing thought, the reference to the concrete instances on the one hand and the relatively abstract marks or meanings on the other is so fundamental that it could not but make itself felt in the earliest scientific analysis of thought, in the Aristotelian logic, though it did not then receive any special denomination. The same lack of definable naming is traceable in the whole scholastic logic. It is only in the 15th Century that some indications of the distinction as having logical significance began to appear, and in modern logic recognition of its value dates from the Port Royal Logic, 1662. Leibnitz, Wolff, and Kant with their followers, as they tried to make the notion the unit of logical thought, naturally assign greatest importance to a distinction which is most clearly evidenced in notions....

Unfortunately, if we use the term "extension" today, it is unlikely that we will be understood. It is especially important that academic, or "ivory-tower" sounding, terms are not used in discussions with executive management. Executive management is always on guard against wasting the resources of the enterprise in unfruitful endeavors, or should be. A simple way to judge this matter is whether people are talking to them in language they can understand. It can pretty much be guaranteed that "extension" will elicit the wrong reaction.

"Scope" is a better term. Even though many people in the average enterprise – including executive management – may not have a very precise understanding of "scope," they will at least know what we are talking about in a general way.

Scope in Data Definitions

From our example above, we can see that we must include scope in data definitions, but what exactly should scope comprise? Once again we are in an area that needs to be worked out more fully, but scope would seem to include the following:

- **Populations or subpopulations of the same things.** The concept that underlies the data object for which we are forming the definition may apply to many things. However, there may be populations of those things that are grouped in some way that has nothing to do with the concept itself. For instance, employees in a global enterprise may be located in many countries. In a particular database table we may wish to include only employees located in one or more countries. We many do this for various reasons, such as common applicability of labor laws, or because we organize human resources departments to cover a particular country or set of countries. All the employees in the enterprise are covered by the concept "employee" but the enterprise can have valid, practical reasons for choosing particular groups to manage in a particular database.

- **Subclasses of a General Concept.** A general concept can often be broken down into specific concepts. In the example given, the concept "employee" was broken down into "permanent employee," "individual contractor," and "subcontractor staff." Each of these specific concepts is dissimilar is a special way, unlike subpopulations of the same things discussed above. We may choose to include or exclude each of these subclasses in the employee data, and that will affect the scope of our data.

- **Collections of Different Things.** Alas, there is nothing to stop a database table being used simply as a storage facility for utterly different things that can somehow

155

be fitted into it. Perhaps the Employee table can have Department or Facility information pushed into it. When this happens the table no longer matches even a single general concept, but is a container for many concepts. Although this situation definitely needs to be recorded under scope in data definitions, it has other implications.

What is Not in Scope

Just as it is important to describe what is in scope in a definition, so it is important to describe what is not in scope. Otherwise, the individual user of the data may be left to infer what is in or out. To do this requires an extremely precise understanding that may not be available from a merely positive definition. It is therefore worth thinking about what populations and subclasses an average user might be aware of, which are not included in the data. These populations and subclasses could then be explicitly listed in the definition as not being within the scope of the data.

Limiting scope in this way is one of the most important contributions that can be made to definitions. In analysis, there is a recurrent problem of the need to state what is absent, and what is excluded from the concept. This is almost never done, and only what is included is stated. The absent and excluded must be captured in the definition, especially if they are significant.

Scope and Attributes

Some may suppose that, at least at the level of a database table, scope can be defined by implementing columns whose values may distinguish the various populations and subclasses that the data covers. So in our **Employee** table example, we may have indicator columns for *Individual Subcontractor, Seconded Canadian Employee*, and so on.

156

There is definite value to this approach, because it shows us the population and subclass a record belongs to. But these columns will be interspersed among many other columns that have nothing to do with the scope of the data, such as *Employee Gender Code, Initial Date of Employment,* and so on. How is any user to distinguish columns that describe scope from columns that do not? Clearly no user should be expected to discover this knowledge unaided. The data definition is the one place where all this information can be described. The columns that can be used to identify the different populations and subclasses can be listed in the definition.

Scope and Difficult Cases

One of the issues with definition is that boundaries tend to remain vague and unsettled in some areas. Two types of circumstance may challenge the definition of scope of data for the enterprise:

- A new instance of something may be encountered and it is unclear if the scope of data means that it should be included or excluded. For instance, in the example of the **Employee** table mentioned above, suppose a Canadian citizen with a valid US immigrant visa applies to become an employee in the US. Should this person be recorded in the US or the Canadian system ?

- The enterprise changes in some way that affects scope. It may be decided that individual contractors will no longer be hired, and that all contractors must work as staff of subcontracting companies.

Part of the problem here is covered by evolution of definitions. However, a significant issue remains. One of the most important cases for the use of definitions is to decide what individual instances are in or out of scope. If a definition is of poor quality, it will be difficult for users to use it. Cases where data users have problems in determining scope should be tracked, because they may well be an indicator of poor definitions.

However, there may be rare, genuinely difficult cases that are not easy to determine even when well-formed definitions are available. There is no reason to expect that such cases will not present themselves from time to time. If these cases are not handled correctly, then the scope as understood in the definition of the data will drift away from the scope as actually contained in the data itself. Eventually this will be recognized and the data will be judged as unreliable. Governance processes are required to keep the definition of data scope in line with the data itself, and these are discussed in the chapter on governance.

Thirteen

Context
of
Data

When writing definitions, we are primarily concerned with concepts, but terms are what signify the concepts, and terms can present problems. We now return to the relationship between definitions and terms, as we consider the problem of context. However, before we get into the issue of context, it is necessary to briefly review synonyms and homonyms.

Synonyms are different terms that signify the same concept, and thus synonyms share the same definition. For instance, a bank might use the terms Bank Client and Bank Customer, both of which would mean

> *an individual who has opened a checking or savings account at the bank.*

Homonyms are different. They are two words that are spelled or pronounced the same but have different meanings, and thus signify different concepts. For instance, *seasoning* can refer to the aging of receivables but can also refer to spices and other flavorings used in food. A company that produces spices will use the term *seasoning* in one way in its accounts receivable unit, but a different way in its manufacturing unit.

Synonyms tend to be thought of in the following ways:

- The definitions that the synonyms refer to completely overlap.

- In every circumstance either one term or the other will be used consistently.

No doubt these assumptions are true in many cases, but there is no law that says they should be. Similarly, there are often simplifying assumptions about homonyms, as follows:

- The concepts that are signified by homonyms are totally distinct, and never overlap.

- The terms that are homonyms can never be synonyms for other concepts.

But in reality there is nothing that forces homonyms to behave in these ways.

Once again we are taking grammar as a point of departure, but when we pass over to data management, we find that the situation is more complex. It is true that data can represent concepts that are totally independent. This is what is expected of the tables in a relational database. Data can also represent concepts that are exactly the same, as when the records in one database table are copied into another table. However, data can also represent concepts that partially overlap. Figure 13.1 illustrates these various situations. (See Fig. 13.1, opposite page.)

Obviously, it is easy to manage independent concepts. It is more difficult to manage synonyms that ultimately refer to the same concept, but it is still reasonably easy to achieve. However, dealing with partially overlapping concepts is much more troubling.

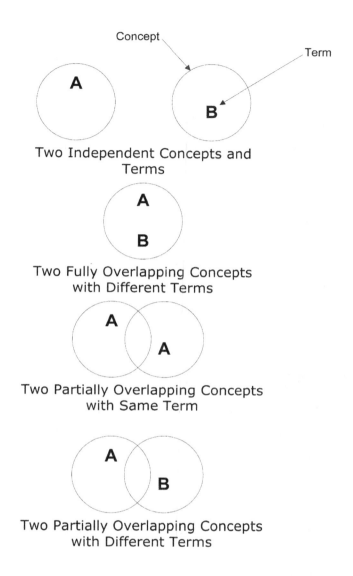

Figure 13.1: *Illustration of Concept Overlap*

Modern database design is founded on the relational theory, which seems to presuppose that all concepts can be identified and do not overlap. How serious can the problem of overlapping concepts be? It can be very serious indeed.

Consider, for instance, the definition of "customer" for an enterprise. The definition of "customer" is often quite difficult to determine, and there may be no single definition for the entire enterprise. For the marketing department, "customer" may include prospects. For the accounts receivable department, a customer is an individual who has purchased something from the enterprise.

Thus we have a concept, termed "customer," which means one thing for the Marketing Department, and a similar, but not identical, thing for the Accounts Receivable Department. However, we have a single, stable, definition of "customer" in the Marketing Department, and a second, stable definition of "customer" in the Accounts Receivable Department. The Marketing Department and the Accounts Receivable Department each represent a context in which the definition of "customer" is modified.

Overlapping Concepts

One of the ways in which we attempt to deal with these difficulties is to consider how terms are stable within contexts. A context can mean the words that surround a term. But it can also mean the circumstances, or setting, in which a term is used. It is the latter meaning that is significant for data management.

Certain concepts have a high degree of definitional overlap, but do not completely overlap. We may be fooled into thinking that these concepts completely overlap because they are often signified by the same term – like "customer." Our experience with dictionaries and the like tends to make us think that concepts either completely overlap (and are represented by synonyms) or are completely different (and are represented by homonyms).

This attitude led early data managers to seek a single definition for every major term used in an enterprise. Generally, any such "search for the single version of the truth," as these exercises were known, was not successful.

To see why such efforts failed, let us consider three definitions of "customer" that might be found in an enterprise:

- **Context of Marketing:** Any individual or enterprise that has, or potentially will, make a purchase from the enterprise.

- **Context of Sales:** Any individual or enterprise that has opened an account with the enterprise.

- **Context of Accounts Receivables:** Any individual or enterprise that owes money to the enterprise or has paid the enterprise.

How do we figure out what the "single definition" might be for the enterprise. It is not even clear from these specific definitions how they could be analyzed to generate a more general, "single," enterprise-wide definition. If we wanted to cover what the three definitions have in common, how would we figure it out? Could someone owe money to the enterprise without opening an account? Could someone potentially make a purchase but not open an account?

Suppose we could answer these questions and work out the common overlap of all these specific definitions. Would such a "definition" satisfy any enterprise-wide needs? Everyone would lose their part of "customer" that did not overlap with every other specific definition. What would be the meaning of what was left? What could be done with it?

However, it is by no means certain that we could figure out the common overlaps and the distinct areas for each specific definition.

There is yet another problem. What is the purpose of an enterprise-wide definition of "customer"? Presumably to report on such high-level information as annual sales per customer, or customer lifetime value, or the average time a customer actively makes purchases from the enterprise. Perhaps one of the specific definitions matches this need better than a generic common overlap.

This is an important consideration because of the insatiable need for enterprises to integrate the data they produce. The idea that all data from an enterprise can be fed into a single data warehouse environment from which business intelligence reporting can be produced is a lot simpler if single terms match single concepts, be they distinct or identical. The idea that we combine a number of subtly different concepts is a good deal more troubling.

Context

If we accept that a general definition of a term such as "customer" can be modified in certain contexts, it becomes important to determine what those contexts are, and how the concept is modified in each of them. These sound like two daunting tasks. Is there any way in which they may be approached?

As of now, there seems to be no foolproof way to identify contexts and track subtle differences in a concept signified by an important term. However, some practical steps can be taken.

The first is to identify the likely areas in an enterprise where commonly used terms refer to subtly different concepts. These may include the following:

- **Subsidiaries.** A subsidiary is a company that is wholly or partially owned by a parent enterprise. Subsidiaries function with some degree of autonomy and may have a distinct culture. A subsidiary's financial results are always carried on the parent's books. Thus, the parent enterprise will need to aggregate data from all subsidiaries in order to understand their relative performance.

- **Lines of business.** A line of business is an organizational structure that supports the overall management of a set of related products and/or services within an enterprise. Sometimes, a line of business may be subject to a special regulatory framework, which is one reason it may be treated separately.

- **Horizontal Business Functions.** A horizontal business function is a unit of an enterprise that provides support across the enterprise for certain administrative functions – for example, Human Resources, Facilities Management, Information Technology.

- **Geographical Locations.** A geographical location is a place where the enterprise has a physical presence. Quite often, geographical locations of an enterprise develop their own cultures, and are strongly influenced by the local culture and legal jurisdiction in which they are situated. Location can affect terms and concepts.

- **Applications.** An application is a computerized system that serves a specific purpose. Often enterprises have many systems that serve the same purpose, and there is no guarantee that all these systems have an identical view of what a common term like "customer" signifies.

Perhaps other items should be included in this list too. The items in this list, or combinations of them, are intended to suggest the possible contexts where shared terms may apply to similar, but subtly different, concepts. Very often, there is a good appreciation of these contexts in the minds of senior management. Ideally, a diagram could be a "cultural map" of the enterprise, showing the potential contexts. I personally have not seen a diagram that addresses all of the items on the above list, and such a diagram may be difficult to produce. Sets of matrices may be an easier approach.

A second practical step is to produce a subject area model. A subject area model is a diagrammatic representation of the most important groups of concepts that the enterprise addresses. It is the highest level of data model, and practice in this area suggests that it should contain 10–20 subject areas. In reality, a subject area model is a taxonomy – a classification of the types of data the enterprise manages from a business perspective. Like all taxonomies it can be debated. As a result, subject area models are prone to being discarded and recreated in the project-driven environment in which data management typically operates. Thus, a subject area model makes most sense where a sustainable data management function has been established. The value of the subject area model is that it should identify concept groups that are widely used across an enterprise. Contained within these groups, therefore, should be the concepts most at risk of varying from one context to another.

When we know – or can guess at – the terms that may refer to concepts that vary from one context to another, we can be more proactive during data integration projects. If any of the candidate concepts are found in such a project, then additional analysis can be undertaken to determine if there is truly one concept arriving from the sources to be integrated, or if there are subtly differing concepts.

Contexts and Definitions

The above approach of formally recognizing contexts can be incorporated in definitions. If we have a definition for "customer," we can include a list of the differing contexts in which the definition is modified, and the corresponding modes of the definition – the ways in which the definition gets modified in each context.

It may be objected that this is not as clean an approach as might be desired. The goal of having one single definition for each concept is violated if we have what amounts to differing concepts included within a single definition. Are we going back to a definition that applies to a term rather than a concept? The problem is that all of our users will use the term "customer" to signify whatever concept they understand by "customer." If we want to separate the concepts out, we will have to invent new terms, such as "Marketing Customer" or "Accounts Receivable Customer" – which nobody uses. This may reduce the usability of our definitions, because users will not be able to find what they want according to the terms they use. Also, splitting out the modified concepts into their own entries risks the loss of the knowledge that these concepts highly overlap and are linked to specific contexts.

Therefore, it may be best to keep single definitions and extend them, to show how modifications of the definition occur in different contexts.

Another data management requirement goes beyond definitions. Suppose we have a database that integrates data from across the enterprise. How does anyone know if a particular customer record in this database is for a "customer" as understood only by Marketing, or as understood by Accounts Receivable, or valid for both. Putting it more generally, does a record represent an instance that is applicable only to one, or some, or all contexts in the enterprise?

Definitions formulated in the way suggested above will tell us the only contexts in which a concept gets modified and the ways in which the context gets modified. This will not help us with any questions about a particular record.

The only way in which this problem can be addressed is to include on a record information about whether the instance represented applies to the distinctive parts of the concept in each context. For example, if a customer record represents a marketing prospect, then a field called *IsProspectIndicator* could be added to the Customer record, and set to a value of "Y" for such a customer. If a customer has paid the enterprise in the past, a field called *HasCustomerPaidIndicator* could be added to their record, and set to a value of "Y" for such a customer. If a customer has closed its accounts, then a field called *IsInactiveCustomer* could be added to the record for the customer and set to "Y." And so on.

It may seem that this approach is somewhat like subtyping, but subtypes must be mutually exclusive. Here we are dealing with very broad overlaps rather than subtypes.

The distinctive indicators can be referenced in the definition of "customer" to show how each applicability can be understood for each "customer" record in context. Once again, we see that the problems of data are not like problems in other areas of human experience, and this highlights the urgency with which it is necessary to better formulate the theory and practice of data management in general.

Fourteen

Sources of Definitions

One of the questions asked about a definition is "Where did it come from?" Knowing the source can provide some degree of assurance about the quality of the definition or may perhaps raise questions about it. Sometimes the definition is contained in a law, in which case the enterprise must use it. In these cases, the source not only validates the definition but adds legitimacy to it by identifying the authority that requires the definition to be used.

However, the term "source" is also used in a rather different way. It can denote the starting point at which we begin to work on a new definition. Using a pre-existing definition, even if it is not of high quality, is always a good idea when trying to formulate a new one. No analyst likes to begin a task with a blank sheet of paper, and it is much easier to determine how a pre-existing definition fails to match a given situation than to start from nothing. More important, this also applies to subject matter experts (SMEs), who must always be consulted when an analyst needs to create a new definition. Asking SMEs to formulate a new definition from scratch puts them in a very awkward position. They are very unlikely to come up with a good one on their first attempt, and whatever they produce will need to be reviewed in any case. This approach will subject them to unwelcome criticism, which could undermine their prestige, and make them significantly more uncooperative in the future. By contrast, if SMEs are presented with a pre-existing definition and asked the criticize it, they run much less personal risk. The natural propensity to criticize rather than create can then be turned to the analyst's advantage because the SME is more willing to provide useful information by pointing out the flaws in an existing definition.

Pre-existing definitions are likely to be found in dictionaries, glossaries, and other documentation. Although these artifacts can be called "sources," they are rather different from a source in the context of a single definition. Thus we need to distinguish between these two uses of "source," and we can change our terminology slightly to do this, as follows:

- **Resource for definitions.** An organization that produces definitions, or a document or equivalent artifact that contains definitions. Knowledgeable individuals can also be considered as resources.

- **Source for a definition.** Within the statement of a definition, this identifies one or more specific locations from which the definition, or elements of it, have been taken.

Resources for Definitions

Resources for definitions are locations from which definitions can be sourced. Resources can be considered from two perspectives. The first perspective is whether they are within the enterprise or outside it:

- **External resource for definitions.** The resource exists outside the enterprise (for example, an online glossary).

- **Internal resource for definitions.** The resource exists within the enterprise (for example, an existing data model).

The second perspective is whether the resource is oriented to definitions:

- Formal Resource. The resource is primarily intended to be a source of definitions (for example, an online glossary).

- Informal Resource. The primary intent of the resource is something other than definitions (for example, design documentation for an application, within which definitions can be found).

An enterprise may have differing degrees of respect or confidence in external versus internal resources, and the same is true of formal versus informal resources. For instance, it may be known that internal documentation is poor, or there may be a distrust of resources that are not primarily oriented to producing definitions. Therefore, it is worth considering categorizing the resources from which pre-definitions may be drawn based on the two schemes described above.

Whatever the characteristics of resources for definitions, they must still be located. The almost reflexive instinct today is to use the Internet to search for resources, and realistically this is probably the major way in which potential sources will be identified. However, Internet search does not guarantee that the best resources will be found, and it does not guarantee that the resources that are found are reliable. Nor does it guarantee that any resource found will be relevant. A resource may be may be good, but it may deal with concepts that do not occur in the enterprise for which the analyst works. Perhaps, as search functionality is better implemented within enterprises, internal resources may be more easily identified.

All this implies that judgments must be made and remembered about the resources. The best way to do this is to maintain a central list of resources. Such a list can be used to quickly access the resources, and user experience with the resources can also be recorded on the list. Such a record will indicate to some extent the value of each resource. It is also possible to indicate on the list if any particular resources should be avoided. It may be possible to go even further and attach metrics for the resources. For instance, a useful metric might be the number of definitions taken from the source.

Maintaining a formal list may help circumvent another occasional issue. One analyst may not share resources with other analysts, in order to maintain some kind of advantage. This kind of behavior is not helpful to the enterprise, irrespective of motive. The result is that individual analysts may not be aware of particular resources, and the knowledge of these sources may be lost over time.

Finally, the list can also function as a checklist. Analysts must sometimes prove their diligence. Showing that all the resources in a fairly extensive list have been consulted for a starting point for a new definition will dispel suspicions among users that the analyst has not done the homework.

Sources and the Enterprise

We now move from resources from which many definitions may be extracted to the source, or sources, for an individual definition. This is where we want to state where the definition came from, and how the source version has been treated. At the level of an individual definition, an enterprise may have several different kinds of relations with a source, as follows:

- **Mandated.** The enterprise is obliged to use a particular source for a definition. This is the case with laws, contracts, regulations, and any other promises that the enterprise must keep.

- **Adopted.** The enterprise uses the definition "as is" from a given source, even though such use is not mandated. One advantage is that the enterprise is effectively outsourcing the maintenance of the definition (if the source is external). Another advantage is that the same source may be used by other organizations that the enterprise deals with, and thus a degree of data integration is guaranteed.

- **Considered.** The enterprise uses the definition as a starting point, and may change it to fit the concept under consideration.

- **Rejected.** The enterprise rejects the source. In analysis, it is always important to capture the fact that something is rejected, and the reason why it has been rejected. This is true with definitions.

Where a definition comes from a mandated or adopted source, then the source must be precisely specified in the definition. This will permit any future analyst to cross-check the definition with the source, and also to determine if the source has changed in any way. It is less vital to show a considered source, but still very useful. Without it, an analyst looking at the definition in the future may wonder if any sources were considered, or if a particular one was, and the analyst may repeat some or all of the work done to arrive at the final version of the definition. All this is also true of a rejected source, which is really just a special case of a considered source.

Authoritative Source

The term "authoritative source" is often used to describe sources used by the enterprise. However, it is an equivocal term, and has a number of meanings, including the following:

- A resource, rather than a source, with a high reputation. The term may refer to the organization that produces the resource.

- A mandated source (see above). The source will consider itself authoritative in this case.

- An adopted source (see above). Here, the enterprise is making the source authoritative with respect to the enterprise. The source may not consider itself authoritative, and if it is external to the enterprise, it may not even be aware of the enterprise.

From this it can be seen that when the term "authoritative source" is used, it can be quite confusing. It is particularly dangerous to say that a *resource* is an "authoritative source." This gives the impression that every definition found in the resource should be adopted by the enterprise, which is far too uncritical an approach.

The term "authoritative source" should not be used to describe resources. It ought only to be used when considering a particular definition, in order to show that the definition was adopted, in its entirety, from the stated source. This will reduce any confusion about what is intended.

Critical Approach

Whatever sources are used, they should be used critically. This includes both mandated and adopted sources. The analyst must try to match the definition provided by the source to the corresponding concept that the analyst is dealing with. First, the definition should be clear. If passages are unclear, they must be analyzed until they are clear, and the analyst must produce a gloss for the definition. This is true even for mandated and adopted definitions. Furthermore, any terms used within the definition must themselves be uniformly understood by all stakeholders in the enterprise.

A danger with taking definitions from sources is that the terms in the definition may be no simpler than the term being defined. For instance, legal definitions can be filled with "legalese" – jargon that only a specialist lawyer can understand. The analyst must then embark on finding definitions for the obscure terms, which leads to an ever-widening circle of even more terms that need defining. This is simply not practical, and the original definition has either to be used "as is," as a reference which is not fully understood, or discarded. Neither choice is good.

A better option for the analyst is to draw on expert help to assist in interpreting the definition. Perhaps the legal department could help. However, expecting this help on a goodwill basis is not realistic or sustainable. The situation points to the need for a governance framework that will extend responsibilities for knowledge management in general. An enterprise cannot claim to be a "knowledge-based organization" (which many claim today) if nobody has any specific responsibilities for knowledge management. However, a good deal of theoretical and practical advances – and probably trial and error – must happen before ways are found to implement knowledge management.

After attempting to clarify terms in the definition, the analyst must next determine how well the definition fits with the concept in the enterprise that the definition is supposed to provide a meaning for. Since the source is presenting the terms, there is no guarantee that any term will really map to the concept it is initially assumed to map to in the enterprise. If the definition is at variance with the meaning of the corresponding concept, then there is a problem. The analyst may need to recommend that another definition be used, or the business be changed to conform to the meaning specified by the definition provided by the source. (This may happen if there is a legal issue.)

There are situations where an enterprise must bring a higher level of analysis to bear on a source. This typically occurs in the reverse engineering of legal documents such as contracts and regulations. Such efforts are not simply an attempt to extract a particular definition from the source, but to fully understand the entire source. The problems with obscure terms mentioned above may require that the reverse engineering include experts, like lawyers, as well as analysts. In these cases it is important to recognize what is required, rather than stumble into such a task without adequate resources. An analyst can be expected to harvest definitions from a source that is not too technical. However, a lone analyst cannot be expected to develop detailed requirements from a source written in highly technical language that happens to contain some definitions.

Turning to considered sources, the analyst will be expected to be even more critical because the formulation of these definitions will inevitably need the participation of subject matter experts (SMEs). SMEs tend to get annoyed with analysts who, in their view, do no work other than asking questions. Engaging an SME without preparing an initial definition is an error. So is engaging an SME with a definition that is simply copied with no attempt to improve its applicability to the enterprise.

The opposite extreme is also encountered at times. In this situation, an analyst thinks that the definition is obvious. Such an analyst may not even bother to look for sources, or when sources are found, the analyst may simply reject the definitions because they do not match the preconceptions of the analyst. Such preconceptions are often based on an analyst's prior work experience. This is a dangerous practice, because the analyst may be rejecting adequate definitions. A better approach is to copy the definitions and then annotate them to suggest improvements – even if this procedure recommends outright rejection. The SMEs who will eventually have to assist in the creation of the definition can then make a judgment on how useful the sources are. The method also demonstrates impartiality on the part of the analyst, which will always raise confidence in the analyst.

The critical approach is perhaps best carried out as follows:

- **Understandability analysis.** The analyst highlights any parts of the definition that are not clear, or are interpreted differently by stakeholders in the enterprise.

- **Gap analysis.** The source may have a definition for a concept that differs from the corresponding concept in the enterprise. The analyst must then recommend changing the definition to make it fit the situation of the enterprise.

- **Level of detail.** The source may be a much more general definition than is adequate for the corresponding concept in the enterprise. It is difficult to argue with general definitions. They are often not wrong, but not very useful. The analyst must suggest detail to be added to the source to make it adequate to the needs of the enterprise.

Citation

Where a definition is taken from a source, the source should be cited. Many definitions are likely to be taken from the Internet, and in that case, the URL and date on which the reference was taken should be captured and stored with the definition. The name of the organization that is responsible for the Web page on which the definition was found should be recorded too, together with any resource (e.g., an online dictionary) housed at that site.

Unfortunately, the Internet is not a stable environment, and anything found on it is subject to change. Therefore, it is probably a good idea to take a screen shot of the Web page where the definition was found and keep the image file with the definition. This is insurance against the organization responsible for the source definition one day deciding to reorganize its Web site or drop the page where the definition was located. Any future analyst looking at the definition can then match it with the source, then and now. This will also safeguard the legacy of the original analyst, because there can be no doubt that the original definition was transcribed faithfully.

The source text should be preserved and marked off from any other text by such devices as italics, different fonts, or enclosure in quotation marks. No reader should be left wondering where the source definition starts and ends in the document the analyst has prepared.

Many sources will derive from the Internet. One way of structuring a citation for such a source would be to put it the URL and the date on which it was last accessed by the analyst in square brackets: [ ]. Square brackets traditionally mean an insertion by the editor, intended to clarify a quotation taken midstream. The term "Source:" can be added to make it clear what the reference means. For instance the definition of "piracy" given in Chapter 6 came from a Web site and may serve as an example:

[Source: *http://www.imo.org/Facilitation/mainframe. asp?topic_id=362*, December 15, 2009]

This is the minimum needed for an Internet citation. Additional elements could include the author, the title of the Web page, the name of the Web site, and the organization responsible for the Web site. These elements should be added if they are of value. In very long web pages it may be necessary to add the paragraph number or heading on the page under which the source definition appeared.

Other than the Internet, citations will most likely be the traditional ones used to refer to printed documentation. There are a number of well-known stylistic conventions. Commonly, they consist of author, year of publication, title of document, location of publication, and publisher. More relevant to definitions are sources from within the enterprise. These sources are likely to be files, not paper documents. In a citation, the exact name of the file, including file type extension should be quoted. Electronic documents are subject to frequent revision, so the version of the document, and the date of its date-time stamp should be quoted. Very often, there is a feeling in most enterprises that documents that have not been recently updated are less trustworthy, so the date-time stamp is particularly important. Even more problematic can be the location of the file. The location must be stated, but file locations are so often changed that the information may not be current. However, this is a problem that affects much more than definitions.

It is possible to place citations in structured metadata – that is, one or more fields related to the definition that are dedicated to citations.

Rejected sources should also be mentioned in definitions, together with the reasons for why they were rejected. This will add confidence to the analysis and prevent any re-examination of the rejected sources. Citations for these sources should also be provided.

Influencing Sources

Today, there are many industry associations and standards bodies. These produce definitions that can be used as sources by an enterprise. It is worthwhile for any enterprise to consider joining such associations and bodies. By joining them, the enterprise may be in a position to influence the formation of definitions that become authoritative sources, and which may in turn affect the enterprise. This is not traditional work for most data managers, who typically have an IT background and are used to building only things that they have been asked to build. The areas of the enterprise outside of IT are usually immature in their attitudes to data, and may not realize how much data constrains and influences the business of the enterprise. Thus, they too are unlikely to engage in any forum where data definitions are created. It is also true that much time may elapse before there is even an opportunity to work on definitions.

However, we are increasingly developing a knowledge-based economy, and enterprises that fully understand this will want to influence the overall information environment for their benefit. Those enterprises that succeed are likely to benefit in the long run. Such activities may seem distasteful to some, but if an enterprise does not represent its own interests, then it should not expect anyone else to represent them either.

Fifteen

Governance
of
Definitions

"Data governance" is the current term used for the management of the enterprise's data resources. It implies setting roles, responsibilities, and rights concerning data. If it is compared, say, with corporate governance, then data governance is currently at a very low level of maturity. For instance, a corporation must have a board of directors, internal and external auditors, highly defined responsibilities with separation of duties, and so on. By contrast, there has been almost no awareness of the need to even manage data in the past, so today there is little understanding of the roles required to manage it, or how it should be managed. Definitions are just one component of the larger problem of data governance. However, even if governance is as yet broadly lacking in most enterprises, some degree of governance cannot be avoided for definitions, nor should we wish to avoid it.

The Need for Openness

One of the main issues with definitions in data management has traditionally been their lack of openness. Definitions have often been stored in repositories that are highly specialized tools that are technically difficult to operate. Perhaps the most common example would be data modeling tools.

The problem with these environments is that they cannot be accessed for reading or update by most of the people who work in the enterprise. Most of the time, the definitions can be accessed only by specialists such as data modelers. It is true that such tools can often export data in a read-only form that can be distributed to the enterprise. However, this approach can create problems. Presenting definitions to the enterprise in general with no possibility of easy change is likely to create resentment. Business users may ask how a small group of data analysts knows so much about the enterprise that they are able to formulate all definitions and present them for general acceptance. Most of the time, the definitions do not even get this far. The data analysts may not have sufficient confidence to publish their definitions. In my experience, analysts rationalize their approach by thinking that the definitions are only for the convenience of a small number of other data analysts and programmers who will be developing applications within the context of tightly bounded projects. Even where definitions are distributed, they are usually contained in "document dumps" with little or no capacity for sorting and searching, and no management of internal relations (such as hyperlinks). Such lack of functionality limits their usefulness.

In summary, there are two common patterns for the distribution of definitions from data analysts:

- (a) Definitions are not widely distributed, but circulated to analysts and programmers involved in developing or supporting applications.

- (b) Definitions are exported from the tools in which they are developed. This is nearly always in a non–updateable form. Little effort is made in the distribution of the definitions beyond placing them in an easily accessible location, and the definitions are not directly updateable.

Neither of these approaches is satisfactory. In this book, it has repeatedly been emphasized that definitions need to be formed with the widest possible collaboration, and must always remain available to further refining. This implies that definitions cannot be managed within an environment that is not accessible by the vast majority of users in an enterprise. Nor can definitions be contained in a tool that is technically difficult to operate. If definitions are widely available, everyone in the enterprise must be able to access them easily and feel that they can add their knowledge to them. Openness must be a principle of definition governance for the long term.

Openness will also facilitate the use of definitions, which is the whole point of investing in them. Definitions must become available as soon as they are developed, and must be accessible in a meaningful way to every user in the enterprise.

Responsibility for Definitions

Openness may present a danger. If nobody in particular has any responsibility for definitions, then nobody will take responsibility for any of them.

The management of definitions is not natural for an individual with an average educational background. This is possibly because current educational systems do not emphasize traditional logic as a tool for use in everyday life. Yet, there are individuals in every enterprise who are very well placed to manage particular definitions because they have the required substantive expertise. It is the task of the data analysts to identify these individuals and match them to definitions to which they are best able to contribute. This is the pattern encyclopedias have followed for many years. The editor of an encyclopedia invites contributors to provide entries on specific topics. Each topic is matched to a specific contributor who is known in advance to have the required expertise.

Such contributors are best thought of as trustees for data definitions. The term "owner" has been used in the literature on data governance, but it gives the wrong impression. "Owner" really means someone who has legal title to something and who can dispose of that thing as seen fit. However, the way the term "owner" has been used in data governance really means a person who takes their responsibilities seriously, as by analogy a true owner should. Frankly, using the term "owner" is a way of evading the need to precisely identify just what these responsibilities are. And of course there cannot be any individuals who hold legal title to any definition in an enterprise, as would be expected of true owners. All definitions belong to the enterprise. Yet, for every definition, one or more individuals should be found who are accountable for the quality and usability of the definition. These individuals can be thought of as "trustees" rather than owners.

A trustee can be assigned a definition, and she or he ideally will ensure that the definition is always of high quality. The only practical way in which data definitions are assigned to trustees would seem to be through analysts. Data and business analysts should be responsible for discovering terms, determining that the terms signify a concept that requires a definition, and then finding individuals in the enterprise who are able to function as trustees for the definition of the concept.

Issues of Trusteeship for Definitions

This is not easy. Data and business analysts have traditionally been able to recognize terms as having special business significance. However, they have typically done this in the context of building a new application for a specific organizational unit of the enterprise, headed by one or a few individuals known as the "business sponsor." A business sponsor is highly motivated to ensure that definitions adequate to the task at hand are provided to the analysts. The task at hand has usually been a project to be completed within a given timeframe. This has tended to make definitions good enough to support the project, has kept the definitions within the circle of the project, and has excluded inputs from the rest of the enterprise. In terms of project management, this is good practice because it reduces dependencies outside of the project and confines scope to the project itself. But it is not intended to help the enterprise at large, nor to persist beyond the implementation of the project. All this could equally be said of other aspects of data governance too, and the reality is that until data governance is fully developed, understood, and accepted, trusteeship for definitions will rely to some extent on the capacity for analysts to interact with the entire enterprise, and the willingness of individuals to act as trustees.

Unfortunately, the project-oriented method is highly ingrained in data and very familiar to business analysts. It is the wrong model for the governance of definitions, because usable definitions must be available to the entire enterprise for an unlimited period of time. The analysts must therefore find ways to identify individuals who can be trustees for definitions, and these individuals must be under an obligation to accept this role.

Breaking Down Trusteeship

A further complication arises when a definition may comprise many parts, and each part may require a different trustee. For instance, a trustee for the business concept portion of a data definition may be a different person from the trustee for the scope of the definition. Perhaps the best way to address this is for the data analysts involved to construct a RACI matrix. "RACI" stands for the roles "Responsible, Accountable, Consulted, and Informed." A RACI matrix matches a set of tasks to a set of individuals or organizational units according to the four roles. An example is presented in Figure 15.1.

	Comptrollers' Office	Internal Audit	Financial Engineering	Data Management
Define business concept	A,R	C	I	I
Scope usage in applications	I	I	I	A,R
Validate definition is correct in all contexts	A	R	R	
Annual review of definition	C	C	C	A,R

Figure 15.1: *Example RACI Matrix*

The definition of each role is as follows:

- **Accountable.** The individual or organizational unit that must ensure the task is carried out successfully. If something goes wrong they will be blamed. Only one "A" per row is accepted.

- **Responsible.** An individual or organizational unit that works on the task at the direction of the "A" party. Ideally, there are one, two, or three "R"s per row.

- **Consulted.** An individual or organizational unit whose feedback is solicited during the task.

- **Informed.** An individual or organizational unit that is told about the task, but whose feedback is not solicited.

The RACI matrix is an excellent way for dividing up the trustee-ship tasks associated with each component of a definition.

General Processes for Definitions

RACI matrices can be used for organizing roles around management tasks for definitions in general, and not just for definition trusteeship. Two other general aspects of data governance are also relevant to a RACI matrix, and these are

- **Individuals and organizational units.** It is necessary to know what these are, how to contact them, and their capabilities.

- **Required tasks.** Just what are the tasks that are needed to manage definitions?

The first point requires data and business analysts to understand the distribution of competencies across the entire landscape of the enterprise. This is not easy, and it is not traditional, in the sense of what analysts have done for years. It must be tackled, but unfortunately, it belongs to a general treatment of analysis that is beyond the scope of this book.

The second point is that the list of tasks required must be developed. It would be nice to have a simple recipe to produce high-quality definitions – a set of steps that could be followed by everyone in any situation. Such "best practices" are frequently demanded from consultants and authors, and often arise from an unwillingness to do any of the hard work of thinking through a particular set of problems on the part of those best placed to do it. This is true in many areas beyond definitions. The reality is that each enterprise must decide on its own priorities, which will influence its requirements for definition management. Fulfilling these requirements will be heavily constrained by the legacy and culture of the enterprise. For instance, some enterprises are start-ups and others are long established. Some have a hierarchical organization, whereas others require consensus building. Therefore, an approach that will work in one enterprise may well fail in another. Each enterprise poses a unique challenge for the analysts that work in it, and part of their job is to understand how to get things done. That said, there are general approaches to definition management, such as trusteeship, that should be adopted, and these general approaches are discussed here.

An Alternative to Trusteeship

Definition trusteeship is not a traditional role. Since the beginnings of wide-scale data management in the 1960s, the emphasis has always been on acquiring or building infrastructure, and the presumption is that technology can meet every need. Hence any attempt to introduce governance for definitions is likely to be met with the response that all that is required is some form of technology. This is especially true of IT management who have carved careers devoted to building and maintaining infrastructure. Today, Wikipedia and similar technologies are often presented as tools that must merely be installed in order to achieve definition management. This simplistic approach can be tempting to senior management, who would often like to see the supposed success of Wikipedia replicated in the enterprise.

There are several major problems with this approach.

- **Participation.** The best instances of success in Wikipedia come when very large numbers of individuals review and contribute to topics. Enterprises simply do not have a large number of people who are sufficiently motivated to contribute. In most enterprises, everyone is already busy and has little capacity for additional work that he or she is not directly asked to perform.

- **Reliability.** Wikipedia itself is not reliable in many specialized areas. Many universities do not permit students to cite it as a source of information. This problem is not addressed simply by implementing Wiki–like technology in an enterprise.

- **Structure.** Enterprises have a hierarchical structure whereas Wikipedia operates on the Internet, where it is open to all individuals without distinction. In an enterprise, a subordinate may be reluctant to criticize an entry made by a supervisor.

From this it can be seen that, without some assignment of trusteeship, definitions may be done in a patchy manner, if at all, and the quality of the definitions is likely to vary.

The Roles of the Trustee

An analyst may provide an initial definition of a concept to a trustee, and list out the terms by which the concept is signified. The definition trustee will then be expected to refine the initial definition of the concept, or the component of the definition of the concept which she or he is assigned. As definitions are published and made available for comment, the trustees must adjudicate the feedback received. That will mean reviewing the feedback and commenting on it, or revising the definition if required.

A project of this sort should not be a particularly onerous task for business users. They will mostly be dealing with the business concept components of definitions, and there are probably hundreds to thousands of such definitions in an enterprise. However, trustees will need some training in definition management and their resulting responsibilities. Providing this training is the responsibility of the analysts. Trustees will also likely need support as they encounter difficulties or unforeseen circumstances in their work. Again, the analysts must provide such support.

While the number of business concepts may not be large, the number of columns in data bases across an enterprise may reach the millions. Many of these are close copies that represent the same business concept. However, they differ in their data-centric aspects, such as the scope of representation. The more technical components of data definitions are much less amenable because they have business users as trustees and business users do not usually have a technical data management background. Hence, both data and business analysts must be trustees for the more data-centric components. It may also be effective to oblige application support teams who implement the database columns to be trustees for the technical components.

Trustees for the technical components of definitions must also handle feedback. They too must comment on it and amend the components for which they are responsible, when necessary.

But what about the scale of the columns in enterprises? Analysts cannot be expected to maintain millions of definitions. However, the number of tables is much smaller, and analysts can be expected to maintain definitions for them. It is at the table level that questions of scope and context are more frequently encountered. Column definitions tend to be less complex with respect to the components that are distinct from the business definition. Hence, one business definition may apply to many columns. In this way the tasks of data trusteeship performed by analysts can be, to some extent, mitigated. It may also be necessary to prioritize the columns allocated to analysts in order to keep workloads reasonable.

Validation and Verification

Despite implementing a trustee-centric governance program for definitions, analysts may still need to get involved if there are disagreements about what a trustee has produced, or if a trustee requires assistance. Generally, if quality is suspected, then a very common practice is to carry out validation and verification. These terms are usually understood as follows:

- **Verification: determining whether** something has been built in accordance with rules, specifications, designs, and so on.

- **Validation:** determining whether something meets its intended purpose.

Both these concepts appear to come from manufacturing environments. "Verification" cannot easily be applied to definitions. Definitions are not built from specifications. In fact, they will often be a basis for specifications. The only way in which verification can be used with definitions is to use it to describe the process whereby a definition is compared to the concept it is supposed to define (or the component of that definition) to determine if it is a match. That has already been discussed in the chapter on producing high-quality definitions. Verification is likely to involve working with the trustee.

"Validation," meaning whether the definition is actually doing the job it was intended for, is also not directly applicable to definitions. A definition is not built to meet a specific purpose, as a toaster is. On the other hand, definitions are needed in data management. But a definition cannot be tested in the same way that a toaster can be tested, by trying to toast different kinds of bread under different conditions. What an analyst can do is identify the stakeholders who are or should be using the definition, and ask to what extent the definition is problematical or useful for these stakeholders. The analyst can also determine if these stakeholders have different views of what the definition should be, in which case there may be a problem of an over-generalized definition, or one that is just wrong.

Taken in the senses just explained, verification and validation are tasks that can be expected of analysts in definition management, and they should be planned for.

Monitoring and Evaluation

Monitoring is the frequent observation of something to determine if it is in an intended or unintended state. It is not a traditional activity in IT, except for monitoring the state of running applications. However, analysts should monitor the degree to which trustees are developing definitions and dealing with feedback, and if issues with definitions are being dealt with in a timely fashion. Successful monitoring depends on the implementation of definitions in an infrastructure where such definitions are easily accessible. Monitoring need not be done constantly, but it should be done periodically, say once a month. It might be interesting to monitor the frequency with which trustees update their definitions, or respond to feedback. An ineffectual trustee could easily be identified and analysts could find out if there is a problem that needs to be resolved.

Monitoring is also useful in that it commits the analyst to obtaining frequent updates on the progress of the definition program. Because definition management is not a traditional activity in data management, and ideally occurs outside of time-bounded projects, monitoring is probably a good idea. The alternative of simply having a project to set up definition management and then allowing definition management to run by itself is much closer to traditional IT management. However, it is likely to fail because of lack of attention and the inability to detect problems as the program is running.

Monitoring is also useful for another aspect of data governance: reporting on the definition management program. In any pioneering activity – which definition management is – the most significant stakeholders will be executive management who have provided the resources and authority for the program. It is essential that executive management hears back from the program at least once a month. They will expect to hear about results more than activities, although activities are important, and they will expect quantitative reporting as well as textual explanations. The analysts running the program must be prepared to report on results.

Evaluation is different from monitoring. It is the determination of the effectiveness of the entire program, and should probably be done only annually. The ideal period is probably in the November-December timeframe of any year, although this will vary for different enterprises. In some enterprises, IT personnel may be wise to coordinate it with the budget cycle. An evaluation will seek to show how the implementation of the definition program has changed outcomes in an enterprise. Showing inputs – the level of resources put into the program – is important, as is showing outputs, which will probably be the number of definitions under management. However, outputs do not demonstrate to executive management, or anyone else, what the program did for the enterprise. It is vital that this information is captured.

An evaluation of a data definition program is probably best made part of an annual report on the state of data governance in the enterprise. Executive management, to whom such a report will always be directed, will appreciate an evaluation of all data management activities in one document that can be consulted at any time. Presenting many smaller documents reduces the importance, and prestige, of each and gives senior managers more complexity to deal with. It will also lead to lack of uniformity in presentation style and content, which may create additional problems. By contrast, a single annual report will avoid such issues.

Metrics

If a data definitions program is to be evaluated, it is important to determine in advance what metrics will measure its effectiveness. As outlined above, the best metrics are those that measure outcomes, not inputs or outputs. If such metrics can be formulated, they will show the real impact of any program to improve data definitions. It is very important to determine what these metrics are, prior to beginning the program to improve definitions, so that they can be baselined. Only if this is done can improvements be accurately measured. If metrics are not considered until after a data definitions program is put in place, then the improvement may be missed and it may be quite difficult to capture the difference that the program has made.

Just what metrics should be captured will differ between enterprises. However, the chapter on why definitions are needed should provide some guidance. Metrics should be expected to vary between enterprises, given that priorities, legacy, and culture vary. It is up to analysts to determine which metrics are appropriate. And of course, metrics must be able to be measured.

Scope Creep

One last item of governance for data definitions is the need to control the scope of the program. Any well-thought-out program for definitions is at risk of additional requirements. Knowledge management is so poor in most enterprises, and the notion of definitions is so weakly understood, that any program that addresses knowledge management in any form may be expected to deliver results that improve knowledge management as a whole. This is not the responsibility of definition management. Expectations need to be clearly set so that that definitions are the only subject of the definitions program, and other areas of knowledge management will not be addressed. It is true that vast areas of knowledge management must be dealt with by all enterprises, but the idea that a definitions program can do this is utterly unrealistic. Analysts need to be on guard against such misperceptions. A vigorous marketing campaign for a definitions program should be undertaken to describe what will be in scope and what will not. How to run such a campaign is beyond the scope of this book, but it is necessary.

Sixteen

Metadata of Definitions

Metadata is often defined as

data about data

This is a particularly unhelpful definition, being too general to provide any understanding of the scope of metadata and containing nothing that is practically actionable. I prefer the following initial definition for metadata:

the data that describes all aspects of an enterprise's information assets, and enables the enterprise to effectively use and manage these assets.

Definitions are metadata because they describe other data that the enterprise manages. Yet in the strange, recursive world of data, definitions do not stand alone. There can be quite important data that describes definitions.

Thus definitions, which are metadata, can have their own metadata. Some data professionals would call this meta-metadata, but the recursion is potentially infinite because anything that ends up as data can have metadata to describe it. If we follow this notion we could have meta-metadata, meta-meta-metadata, meta-meta-meta-metadata, and so on.

Clearly such an outcome is not useful. The approach taken in this book is that data represents something else, but data is also a thing in its own right that can be described by other data. The "something else" that data represents can, therefore, be other data. On this view we end up with a network of relationships, rather than a hierarchy. Sometimes it seems that data professionals who believe in such a hierarchy want it to have a fixed number of levels, as if metadata were bounded in some way. In reality, metadata is unbounded, just like data.

While we should not limit ourselves in thinking about metadata for definitions, it is also true that there is a fairly stable set of metadata that will probably apply to most definitions. It is worth examining this metadata, much of which is bound up with how definitions are managed.

Dublin Core Metadata

When discussing metadata, a standard that is frequently raised is the Dublin Core Metadata, which is defined as follows:

> The Dublin Core Metadata Initiative, or "DCMI," is an open organization engaged in the development of interoperable metadata standards that support a broad range of purposes and business models.
> [Source: http://dublincore.org/, December 15, 2009]

The Dublin Core set of 15 metadata items, that are metadata entity types. They are more fully described in *Appendix 2,* but can be summarized as

1. Contributor

2. Coverage

3. Creator

4. Date

5. Description

6. Format

7. Identifier

8. Language

9. Publisher

10. Relation

11. Rights

12. Source

13. Subject

14. Title

15. Type

The definition of the DCMI is extremely vague, and this is partly why it seems to be considered as a starting point in many discussions about metadata. It is also oriented to library science, and publications, which many also feel is closely related to definitions, perhaps once again because dictionaries are associated with definitions and dictionaries are publications.

Probably the only items worth considering in the DCMI are **Contributor, Creator,** and **Source. Coverage** – spatial and temporal properties – does not apply to most concepts. **Date,** by itself, is not meaningful. **Description** is not relevant, because a definition is often a description. **Format** is relevant only for some technical aspects. **Identifier** basically means a surrogate key, and that is an implementation option. **Language** is not something that must be dealt with in most circumstances. **Publisher** is not relevant to an enterprise. **Relation** is far too vague, and is actually an Aristotelian category. **Rights** are again not relevant to an enterprise, which owns all the metadata. **Subject** is not relevant to a definition, as the definition tries to explain its subject. **Title** is not relevant as the definition is trying to explain what is meant by one or more terms that are known in advance. **Type** is an extremely vague term, and if we look further into it, it appears that it is not anything that applies specifically to definitions.

Contributor is of interest, because many individuals will be expected to contribute to definitions. **Creator** is of some interest, because some definitions may be data entered by a particular individual. **Source** is very interesting because some definitions may have sources outside of the enterprise, and other definitions may be obtained from documents within the enterprise.

We have examined the Dublin Core Metadata in some detail because it is one of the few metadata standards that exist and executive management in many enterprises know of it. Whatever uses the DCMI has, it would appear to be limited with respect to the management of definitions.

Definition Metadata

It is very unlikely that a single pattern for definition management metadata that an enterprise can simply adopt will emerge. Ideally, every enterprise should clearly articulate the business drivers that determine its requirements for definition management, and use those drivers as a basis for detailed design. The attitude that some pre-existing solution merely needs to be selected can be an excuse for avoiding the work needed to gain agreement on the business drivers, formulate the requirements, and do the design. On the other hand, definition management is still a relatively immature area, and enterprises can benefit from examining examples of designs that are available. Such designs can be compared to the situation in an enterprise and can be used to understand how certain requirements may or may not be met.

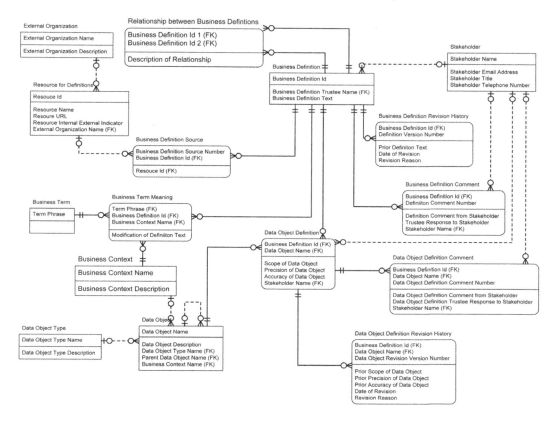

Figure 16.1: *Data Model for Definition Metadata*

In that spirit, a possible logical model of definition metadata is presented in Figure 16.1. A fuller description of the model is provided in Appendix 3. The model is not intended for adoption by any specific enterprise. Rather it illustrates some of the topics discussed in this book. It is also simplified in order to highlight key topics, and, as will be shown below, there are many additional detailed considerations that must be factored into any data model for definition management. We will now examine the major areas in Figure 16.1.

Stakeholder

One of the first things to note is a list of stakeholders. The entity type **Stakeholder** does that in Figure 16.1. **Stakeholder** is designed to hold information about individuals. Individuals have roles, responsibilities, and rights in definition management. It may well be necessary to extend this part of the design to show which organizational unit an individual belongs to. Interestingly, in every aspect of data governance there is a need for stakeholder information. This is not simply a requirement of definition management. Its immediately raises the issue of whether a central list of stakeholders should be maintained that can be accessed by all applications involved in governance, or whether (as is shown here) there should be one copy of such a list per application. This issue really belongs to the domain of master data management (MDM) rather than definition management. It needs to be dealt with carefully, but is outside the scope of this book.

Once it is understood that **Stakeholder** is a type of master data (or perhaps master metadata) it is obvious that historical versions must be managed. After all, master data is about things, and things change. This is not shown in Figure 16.1, but in the long run it will be necessary. However, changed data capture is not easy to implement, and if we put it into an application intended for definition management, the application will start to look more like an application for stakeholder management.

This argues that stakeholder metadata should be maintained outside the definition management metadata, and simply made available to the definition management application, even if redundancy is controlled. It is also evident that a data governance program that includes stakeholder management should exist prior to, or run parallel with, definition management. Further, the general problems of master data management illustrated here must also be tackled by the enterprise. They should not be solved on an ad hoc basis within a program intended for definition management. At least a common approach to these problems should be agreed upon.

These kinds of intertwining issues are a constant reality in data management, so it should not be surprising that they are found in definition management. There are no easy answers. Their mutual interdependence means that it is impossible to wait until all dependences are understood and dealt with, because that will never happen. A more practical approach is to develop a long-range plan and implement simple but useful functionality at first. Where difficulties arise, such as stakeholder history, these may have to be dealt with manually by analysts until eventually the required functionality is built. The perfect cannot be the enemy of the best, or even the good. Thinking that every last detail can be worked out in advance will only lead to consideration of ever-widening circles of dependent components and result in analysis paralysis. Definition management may be prone to this problem because it is different and not many people are experts at it.

External Organization

Like **Stakeholder, External Organization** is also master data. It is probably less important because fewer external organizations are likely to be involved in processes around definition management. Instead they are more likely to be referred to. However, they can sometimes be very important. As has been discussed, some external organizations may create definitions that must be adhered to. For instance, regulatory agencies often define concepts that they require enterprises to report on. In these cases, the enterprise will need to monitor the external organization to determine if it has changed any definitions. Perhaps there are services provided by an external organization that an enterprise can subscribe to. Metadata for monitoring is not included in Figure 16.1, but is certainly worth considering. What is more important is that External Organization is an entity type that should occur in any data model for definition metadata.

Business-Centric and Data-Centric Metadata

Figure 16.1 uses a design pattern whereby definitions of business concepts are held separately from definitions of data objects. **Business Definition** is used to contain definitions of business concepts that are then mapped to **Business Term** using the association entity type **Business Term Meaning**. This will provide glossary functionality that permits synonyms and homonyms in the business terms.

The data objects are represented first by **Data Object Type**, which lists the different kinds of data objects that can exist, for example, "Entity Type," "Table," "Report Label" and so on. Then the **Data Object** is designed to hold information about the actual data objects, for example, a entity type, or table, or report label.

Each **Data Object** has a detailed definition that is held in **Data Object Definition**, which is also a child of **Business Definition**. Thus there is no need to repeat a business definition independently for each data object that must be defined. Maintaining definitions for the same business concept independently in definitions of many data objects is very difficult. This design avoids it.

Data Object Definition also separates components of data-centric definitions. Scope, precision, and accuracy are all called out as separate attributes of **Data Object Definition**. Thus a user can go straight to information about scope, instead of having to extract it from a more general definition text.

Comments

Both **Business Definition** and **Data Object Definition** have child entity types that are intended to allow comments to be added to each definition. This means that the definitions are left intact until their trustees modify them. Furthermore, it less risky for any user to create a comment except in order to directly modify a definition.

This lack of risk will hopefully encourage staff across the enterprise to contribute their thoughts and experience to definitions.

History

For purposes of monitoring and evaluation, it is necessary to track all revisions to definitions, that is, the revision history. The entity types **Business Definition Revision History** and **Data Object Revision History** achieve this objective. It is tempting to simply leave out this aspect of definition management and keep only the current version of definitions. This is a valid option and may be a reasonable position at the beginning of definition management.

Ultimately, over time, it will be necessary to understand how definitions have changed and why they have changed. The review of such changes is an important function of the overall data governance function that must exist to assure the high quality of data definitions.

Conclusion

We have examined a very rudimentary model for the metadata of definition management. What is critically important is the need to design stores of metadata for definitions. If this is not done, then definitions will simply be large text blocks from which components, such as scope or accuracy, cannot be easily extracted. It will be difficult to implement processes such as the supervised incorporation of feedback. Unnecessary redundancy, such as the repetition of business definitions, will also be necessary.

Structured metadata will allow for richer and more complex functionality in definition management. It will also force definitions to be implemented in a true database rather than content in electronic documents. This cannot perhaps be achieved quickly in definition management, but it should be a long-term goal.

Seventeen

Conclusion

We have now surveyed definitions in the context of information management. To a large extent we have considered definitions with respect to the narrower field of data management. But "information management" is broader than "data management" and conveys what the overall purpose of "information technology" is – or should be. Definitions can be proven (or at least strongly argued) to be important for information management, but is that proof simply theoretical or does it really matter in practice?

For many, there will remain nagging doubts about whether definitions really are important. After all, it is not easy to find examples of the practical value of definitions in ordinary life. People just do not seem to discuss them much. This must inevitably lead us to question the extent to which definitions are relevant in information management.

This brings us back to where we started – the justification of definitions – and it is worth looking a little more deeply into why definitions may have a special role in information management that is different from the role they play in ordinary life. Once again, this may be particularly applicable to dealing with executive management. Because executive management are not experts in everything they must deal with, they will tend to use their personal experience, often thought of as "common sense," to assess how they should make decisions. If definitions have little or no role in their personal lives, executive management may be cautious about any claims that definitions are necessary for information management. On the other hand, definitions often matter in resolving problems, such as who is responsible for something, and experience of this may favorably dispose executive management to definitions management.

How Important Are Definitions?

The role of definitions in ordinary life does indeed seem to be limited. We do not need definitions to be able to peel a banana or drive a car. We need to be told what things are called, how they work, and what we can do with them, but this is not quite the same as a definition. Often, it seems that we cannot really appreciate a definition and need to experience something to understand it. The first time I ate pastrami was the first time I really knew what it was, despite having had it described to me beforehand several times.

So if we can get along in our daily routines with only infrequent assistance from definitions, why is the same not true of information management?

The answer seems to lie in what information management deals with. In our ordinary lives we interact with – for want of a better word – "reality." Reality is the world composed of matter and energy – all the "things" around us that we can see, touch, feel, taste, and smell. These things generally behave themselves without our help. That is, they obey the laws of natural science, mathematics, and indeed metaphysics, without human efforts to enforce such laws. We ourselves can manipulate the real world, but still only within the boundaries set for us by the same sets of laws that govern the rest of reality. In one way, this is annoying, because quite often we do not like the results of these laws – such as getting old. In another way, it is quite convenient because unless we choose to manipulate reality, it is quite capable of looking after itself and we need not work to keep it going.

But besides that external reality, there is a "world" based on ideas which, for our own reasons, we have created. This is the world of overdrafts, mortgages, shares of ownership, asset-backed securities, insurance policies, credit default swaps, debt instruments, corporations, loans, product lines, and the like. None of these are built from atoms and energy in the same way as natural objects are. Yet they exist. Take an overdraft, for instance. It is not a piece of paper that I receive from the bank. That is only a signal that the overdraft exists. And it exists because the bank, the laws of the jurisdiction in which I live, and – unfortunately – I myself all agree that the overdraft exists. I can try to dispute with the bank that I actually have an overdraft at the present time, but I would be very foolish indeed to suggest that the concept of an overdraft does not exist, so that nobody could ever have one. Everyone knows what an overdraft is, and that overdrafts are possible. But unlike roses and tables, we do not get to know about overdrafts by perceiving them. We must have them explained to us – we have to understand their definition.

Information technology has allowed us to build environments that are like farms where we can create and manage things like overdrafts that are purely conceptual. Prior to the Information Age, this work had to be done all by hand, just as craftsmen produced manufactured goods prior to the Industrial Age. But in the IT environment we have the responsibilities of creators, which we do not have in a material environment. A banana will look after itself. An overdraft will not. We have to say what an overdraft is and how it behaves. We can then create overdrafts under the conditions we have specified, and process them according to rules that we have specified. Perhaps an overdraft occurs when a negative balance persists in an account past close of business on any day, and perhaps there is a $35 fee for incurring an overdraft and a daily charge of 0.83 percent on the amount of the negative balance until it disappears. In other words, people cannot understand what an overdraft is until they have a definition of it. For myself, I must know in general terms what it is, but for the developers who create the applications in which overdrafts are processed, the definition must be complete. Failure to do this will mean that overdrafts will not be processed according to their legal specification. The overdrafts will not simply look after themselves. We have created the technology in which we can automate the management of vast numbers of overdrafts to replace clerks, quill pens, ink, ledger books, and sloping desks. But we have had to assume the mantle of creators in these new environments. Definitions are an integral part of the responsibilities of being a creator – in making our virtual worlds run smoothly.

Everyone who works with data long enough, and reflects on what they are doing with it, eventually gets the uncomfortable feeling that he or she is not dealing with something that is "real." In this chapter, I have tried to provide my personal analysis of the situation, which I think helps us understand why definitions are so much more important in information management than in other departments of human experience. I have done this because I have found no satisfactory explanations produced by "information science" that I can use as a foundation to justify to executive management why they should invest some resources in definitions in information management, given that definitions are not a major part in the everyday life of the average executive. Perhaps I am mistaken in my analysis, and I would welcome any correction. However, I am certainly disappointed that "information science" has not addressed the issue in much detail.

Definition as Product and Process

Articulating the reasons why definitions are especially necessary and valuable in information management is one thing. However, we must also overcome the preconception that definition is only about statements of definitions – metadata objects. Anyone expected to work with definitions, or fund such work, must appreciate that, while definitions may be objects, definition is itself a process – and not a trivial one.

Once again, we must remind ourselves that definition management in the depth advocated here is not traditional in data management, and certainly not in ordinary life. As such, it will be a pioneering activity wherever it is carried out. In any enterprise, the most important stakeholders for any pioneering activity will be the executives who invest the resources in it. It is these stakeholders that data managers must keep satisfied, and part of the task is to anticipate their attitude to the specific proposal. The idea of definition as process is not likely to be natural to them.

Probably the most common experience of the process of definition in ordinary life is when we come across a term we don't recognize and "look it up." We may tend to assume that many definitions are simply "out there somewhere" waiting to be gathered. We have already seen that specialized concepts are very common in all enterprises, and while starter definitions may exist, they may need to be considerably modified and augmented to truly fit the concepts to be defined. This situation implies that one or more processes should be put in place to obtain the desired result.

Executive management probably needs some examples of how the process would work before agreeing to allocate any resources. The examples offered need not be precise, but they must demonstrate that some complex processes are inevitable, and that work will be required to specify them fully. This is the sort of thing that executives can appreciate.

A little more difficult, however, is the understanding that definition is a continuing process. Executives are likely to think that definitions are produced as in a dictionary, and that is the end of the matter. The dictionary is kept up to date with the addition of new terms or when existing terms acquire new meanings. However, as we have seen, definitions are much more complex in data management. They have data-centric aspects that must be captured. For instance, if the report label "Customer" on Report XYZ filters out customers that have not made purchases in the past 18 months, we need to know. As new applications are developed, as bugs are found in existing ones, and as knowledge in general slowly diffuses across the enterprise, it is necessary to update definitions to store everything useful the enterprise is aware of in them. Nor can all of this be left unmanaged. Governance, including trusteeship, monitoring, and evaluation must be put in place and run for the indefinite future. Definitions will be unsustainable if they are simply carried out in the context of a single time-bounded project.

All of this is different from the traditional practice of IT over the past several decades. However, as data management matures, the realization is growing that the old ways of IT no longer apply. The problem is that these ways are highly ingrained, and there are few generally accepted methodologies in data management – at least relative to the demands of the discipline. There seems to be a growing tension between the traditional approach of IT – to build, implement, and maintain infrastructure – and data management which must focus on data content. Where this is leading us is not yet clear. But what is clear is the enormous reversal that has occurred since the 1960s, when the focus of information systems was on automation of business processes and data was thought of as merely their byproduct. Today the emphasis is on data itself, and much less so on automation. Definitions are the fundamental metadata of meaning for the data resource, and they must play a central role as we move into a more data-centric world. It is high time that information management works out a much improved theoretical and practical answer to this need.

Appendix 1:
Glossary of Common Data-Management Terms

The following are brief nominal definitions for some common terms used in data management.

Application. A computerized system that is oriented to the management of information.

Analyst. An individual who is responsible for understanding a situation. Analysts can document (among other things) general requirements for a computerized application, items of functionality that are needed by an application, how existing processes work, how business users wish future processes to work, and tests to be performed on an application to determine if it meets its requirement. Today, analysts fall into two broad areas: data analysts who concentrate on data and business analysts who concentrate on processes.

Attribute. A characteristic of an entity type in a data model.

Business. The part of the enterprise that is located outside the IT department. The mindset that partitions an enterprise into "the business" and "IT" is increasingly being seen as counter-productive, and the division may not long endure.

Column. In a relational database, a column holds (or should hold) a single item of information, corresponding to an attribute of an entity type. The meaning of this column should be the same in every record of the table.

Database. A store of related data

Data Model. A technique, usually diagrammatic, used to design or document the structure of a database.

Designer. An individual who takes the outputs of an analyst and creates a plan for a solution to fulfill the requirements that have been captured by the analyst. The designer must be very familiar with the tools available to build the solution and must manage the inevitable trade-offs that occur when planning the solution. Sometimes the analyst and designer are the same person, but the required skill sets are usually so different that this is comparatively rare.

Entity Type. A concept that is of interest to the enterprise, and for which it is desired that information will be managed.

Enterprise. An organization that is autonomous in terms of managing its information processing environment. It may be for-profit or not-for-profit, as in the case of government. Autonomy in terms of maintaining an information-management environment may not equate to other kinds of autonomy. For instance a subsidiary may be expected to maintain its own information-processing environment, but may be directed to some extent in how it should do this by a parent company.

Field. An instance of a data structure in which a single value can be placed. A record is said to have fields. Fields can occur in data structures that are not necessarily relational databases.

User. An individual who has to consume information maintained in an application as assigned tasks are carried out. Usually it has meant business user, which is an individual working outside the IT department. As IT staff also begin to rely on applications, so the term has been expanded to include IT users.

Appendix 2:
Dublin Core Metadata

The table below presents the 15 items in the Dublin Core Metadata. See Chapter 16 for a discussion of their relevance.

Item	Name	Definition
1	Contributor	An entity responsible for making contributions to the resource. Examples of a Contributor include a person, an organization, or a service. Typically, the name of a Contributor should be used to indicate the entity.
2	Coverage	The spatial or temporal topic of the resource, the spatial applicability of the resource, or the jurisdiction under which the resource is relevant. Spatial topic and spatial applicability may be a named place or a location specified by its geographic coordinates. Temporal topic may be a named period, date, or date range. A jurisdiction may be a named administrative entity or a geographic place to which the resource applies. Recommended best practice is to use a controlled vocabulary such as the Thesaurus of Geographic Names (TGN). Where appropriate, named places or time periods can be used in preference to numeric identifiers such as sets of coordinates or date ranges.

Item	Name	Definition
3	Creator	An entity primarily responsible for making the resource. Examples of a Creator include a person, an organization, or a service. Typically, the name of a Creator should be used to indicate the entity.
4	Date	A point or period of time associated with an event in the lifecycle of the resource. Date may be used to express temporal information at any level of granularity. Recommended best practice is to use an encoding scheme, such as the W3CDTF profile of ISO 8601 (W3CDTF).
5	Description	An account of the resource. Description may include but is not limited to an abstract, a table of contents, a graphical representation, or a free-text account of the resource.
6	Format	The file format, physical medium, or dimensions of the resource. Examples of dimensions include size and duration. Recommended best practice is to use a controlled vocabulary such as the list of Internet Media Types (MIME).
7	Identifier	An unambiguous reference to the resource within a given context. Recommended best practice is to identify the resource by means of a string conforming to a formal identification system.
8	Language	A language of the resource. Recommended best practice is to use a controlled vocabulary such as RFC 4646 (RFC4646).

Item	Name	Definition
9	Publisher	An entity responsible for making the resource available. Examples of a Publisher include a person, an organization, or a service. Typically, the name of a Publisher should be used to indicate the entity.
10	Relation	A related resource. Recommended best practice is to identify the related resource by means of a string conforming to a formal identification system.
11	Rights	Information about rights held in and over the resource. Typically, rights information includes a statement about various property rights associated with the resource, including intellectual property rights.
12	Source	A related resource from which the described resource is derived. The described resource may be derived from the related resource in whole or in part. Recommended best practice is to identify the related resource by means of a string conforming to a formal identification system.
13	Subject	The topic of the resource. Typically, the subject will be represented using keywords, key phrases, or classification codes. Recommended best practice is to use a controlled vocabulary. To describe the spatial or temporal topic of the resource, use the Coverage element.
14	Title	A name given to the resource. Typically, a Title will be a name by which the resource is formally known.

Item	Name	Definition
15	Type	The nature or genre of the resource. Recommended best practice is to use a controlled vocabulary such as the DCMI Type Vocabulary (DCMITYPE). To describe the file format, physical medium, or dimensions of the resource, use the Format element.

[Source: Source: http://dublincore.org/, December 15, 2009]

Appendix 3:
Elements of Preliminary
Metamodel for Definitions

The preliminary data model for definitions was discussed in Chapter 16. Only initial definitions of the elements in the model are presented here. In an actual implementation, full definitions would be needed. The model diagram is reproduced for ease of reference.

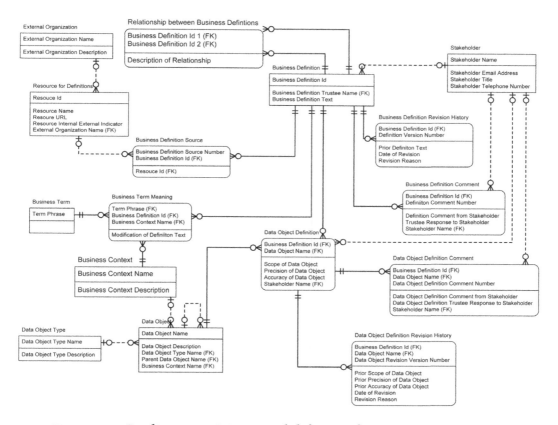

Figure A3.1 *Preliminary Metamodel for Definition Management*

Entities

Business Context. A defined area of the enterprise within which a **Business Term** signifies a concept that is somewhat (but not totally) different from how that concept is understood elsewhere in the enterprise. The context may be related to culture, organizational unit, legal jurisdiction, and so on. Often one context will have modified definitions for many concepts.

Business Definition. The definition of a concept that is relevant to the enterprise, but which is completely abstracted away from any element of how it is implemented in information technology.

Business Definition Comment. Any feedback from a stakeholder on a **Business Definition**. It is up to the definition trustee to determine if this feedback will be incorporated into the definition.

Business Definition Revision History. All the changes that have been applied to a **Business Definition.**

Business Definition Source. A **Resource for Definitions** from which a **Business Definition** is taken. It may be modified from the definition in the source. This is probably inadequate for tracking sources that are not strictly resources. The model does not have a way of tracking sources for **Data Object Definitions**, which is another weakness.

Business Term. A word or phrase used in the enterprise to signify a concept that is of interest to the enterprise. A **Business Term** can be a synonym and/or a homonym.

Business Term Meaning. An association between **Business Term, Business Context,** and **Business Definition.** It is the definition that applies to a given term in a given context. It also allows a given term to have more than one meaning in a given context.

Data Object. An instance of a **Data Object Type** – for example, a particular database table, a particular report, a particular entity type in a particular data model.

Data Object Definition. The definition of any **Data Object.** This is taken to have a single Business Definition and a number of data-centric components.

Data Object Definition Comment. Any feedback from a stakeholder on a **Data Object Definition**. It is up to the definition trustee to determine if this feedback will be incorporated into the definition.

Data Object Definition Revision History. All the changes that have been applied to a **Data Object Definition**.

Data Object Type. Any type of structural component of a data store, or any type of output of an application where data is presented, for example, database table, report. Additionally it includes metadata objects, which are types of component of metadata stores, for example, entity types in data models, business concept definitions in glossaries.

External Organization. A legal entity that is not part of the enterprise that is undertaking definition management, nor any parent or subsidiary organization of the enterprise. Thus the external organization is autonomous in terms of the way it manages information, including definitions.

Relationship Between Business Definitions. Any two **Business Definitions** can have a relationship. A disadvantage of the design here is that only two instances of a relationship are permitted. A better design might allow an unlimited number of instances.

Resource for Definitions. A publication of some kind that contains many definitions, for example, an online glossary. It may be external or internal. If external, it is produced by an **External Organization.**

Stakeholder. An individual who has a defined role, or rights, or responsibility with respect to definition management. One weakness of the design here is that organizational units are not considered. Another is that it is implied that all stakeholders exist within the enterprise. A different design might question these aspects.

Attributes

Business Context. *Business Context Name.* A unique name assigned to a **Business Context.** It should be descriptive and, if possible, not be a new term.

Business Context. *Business Context Description.* An explanation of how the **Business Context** may be recognized and why it is important for definition management.

Business Definition. *Business Definition Id.* A surrogate key that is used to identify a **Business Definition.** Terms cannot be used as they can be equivocal.

Business Definition. *Business Definition Text.* The definition of a business concept. This is a core item of knowledge that is being managed.

Business Definition. *Business Definition Trustee Name.* The name of the stakeholder who acts as the trustee for the **Business Definition.**

Business Definition Comment. *Business Definition Id.* The identifier of the **Business Definition** for which a comment is made.

Business Definition Comment. *Definition Comment Number.* A sequential number that is incremented for each new comment.

Business Definition Comment. *Definition Comment from Stakeholder.* The text of a comment on the **Business Definition** provided by a **Stakeholder.**

Business Definition Comment. *Stakeholder Name.* The name of the **Stakeholder providing the comment.**

Business Definition Comment. *Trustee Response to Stakeholder.* Any reply by the trustee of the **Business Definition** to the comment made by the **Stakeholder.**

Business Definition Revision History. *Business Definition Id.* The identifier of the **Business Definition** for which history is being tracked.

Business Definition Revision History. *Version Number.* A number that is incremented every time a new revision is made to the **Business Definition.**

Business Definition Revision History. *Prior Definition Text.* The **Business Definition.** *Business Definition Text* before it was changed to make the next version.

Business Definition Revision History. *Date of Revision.* The date on which the **Business Definition.** *Business Definition Text* was changed and a new version made.

Business Definition Revision History. *Revision Reason.* A description of why the definition was changed.

Business Definition Source. *Business Definition Id.* The identifier of the **Business Definition** for which a source is being associated.

Business Definition Source. *Source Number.* A sequential number that is incremented for every source that a given **Business Definition** has.

Business Definition Source. *Resource Id.* A sequential number representing a resource that is a source for a given **Business Definition.**

Business Term. *Term Phrase.* A word or group of words used to signify a business concept that must have a Business Definition.

Business Term Meaning. *Term Phrase.* A term that is being associated with a **Business Definition** and **Business Context.**

Business Term Meaning. *Business Definition Id.* A surrogate key that is used to identify the **Business Definition** that is being associated with the term in the context.

Business Term Meaning. *Business Context Name.* The name of the context within which the term has a given definition.

Data Object. *Data Object Name.* The technical identifier of the **Data Object.**

Data Object. *Data Object Description.* A description of where the **Data Object** is located.

Data Object. *Data Object Type Name.* The **Data Object Type** that this **Data Object** is an instance of.

Data Object. *Parent Data Object Name.* If the **Data Object** exists within another **Data Object,** this is the identifier of the parent **Data Object.**

Data Object. *Business Context Name.* Optionally indicates if the **Data Object** is used within a particular **Business Context.**

Data Object Definition. *Business Definition Id.* A surrogate key that is used to identify the **Business Definition** that is related to the **Data Object.**

Data Object Definition. *Data Object Type Name.* The unique identifier of the **Data Object Type** for which a data-centric definition is being provided.

Data Object Definition. *Scope of Data Object.* A description of the coverage of the data object. This is part of the data-centric definition of the **Data Object.**

Data Object Definition. *Precision of Data Object.* A description of the actual numeric tolerances of the data object. Applies only to quantitative aspects of the **Data Object.** This is part of the data-centric definition of the **Data Object.**

Data Object Definition. *Accuracy of Data Object.* A description of the extent to which the data object actually represents what it is supposed to represent. This is part of the data-centric definition of the **Data Object.**

Data Object Definition. *Stakeholder Name.* The name of the Stakeholder who is the trustee for the **Data Object Definition**.

Data Object Definition Comment. *Business Definition Id.* The identifier of the **Business Definition** associated with the **Data Object** for which a comment is made.

Data Object Definition Comment. *Data Object Name.* The identifier of the **Data Object** for which a comment is made.

Data Object Definition Comment. *Data Object Definition Comment Number.* A sequential number that is incremented for each new comment.

Data Object Definition Comment. *Data Object Definition Comment from Stakeholder.* The text of a comment on the **Data Object** provided by a **Stakeholder.**

Data Object Definition Comment. *Stakeholder Name.* The name of the **Stakeholder** providing the comment.

Data Object Definition Comment. *Trustee Response to Stakeholder.* Any reply by the trustee of the **Data Object Definition** to the comment made by the Stakeholder.

Data Object Definition Revision History. *Business Definition Id.* The identifier of the **Business Definition** associated with the **Data Object** for which a history is being tracked.

Data Object Revision History. *Data Object Name.* The identifier of **Data Object** for which history is being tracked.

Data Object Revision History. *Version Number.* A number that is incremented every time a new revision is made to the **Data Object Definition.**

Data Object Revision History. *Prior Scope of Data Object.* The **Data Object Definition.** *Scope of Data Object* before it was changed to make the next version.

Data Object Revision History. *Prior Precision of Data Object.* **The Data Object Definition.** *Precision of Data Object* before it was changed to make the next version.

Data Object Revision History. *Prior Accuracy of Data Object.* **The Data Object Definition.** *Accuracy of Data Object* before it was changed to make the next version.

Data Object Revision History. *Date of Revision.* The date on which the **Data Object Definition** record was changed and a new version made.

Data Object Revision History. *Revision Reason.* A description of why the **Data Object Definition** record was changed.

Data Object Type. *Data Object Type Name.* A unique name that can be used to identify a **Data Object Type.**

Data Object Type. *Data Object Type Description.* A definition for a **Data Object Type.**

External Organization. *External Organization Name.* The official name of the **External Organization.**

External Organization. *External Organization Description.* A description of the **External Organization.**

Relationship Between Business Definitions. *Business Definition Id 1.* One identifier of the two **Business Definitions** in a relationship.

Relationship Between Business Definitions. *Business Definition Id 2.* The second identifier of the two **Business Definitions** in a relationship.

Relationship Between Business Definitions. *Description of Relationship.* The nature of the relationship between the two **Business Definitions.**

Resource for Definitions. *Resource Id.* A surrogate key that uniquely identifies a **Resource for Definitions.**

Resource for Definitions. *Resource Name.* The name for a **Resource for Definitions.** Ideally this will be the official name.

Resource for Definitions. *Resource URL.* Optionally the URL where a **Resource for Definitions** can be found, or information on it can be found.

Resource for Definitions. *Resource Internal External Indicator.* An indicator that shows whether the resource is maintained within the enterprise or external to it.

Resource for Definitions. *External Organization Name.* Where *Resource Internal External Indicator* is "External," this is the name of the **External Organization** responsible for the resource.

Stakeholder. *Name.* The name of an individual who can be a **Stakeholder.**

Stakeholder. *Email Address.* The email address of an individual **Stakeholder.**

Stakeholder. *Title.* The official title of the **Stakeholder** within the enterprise.

Stakeholder. *Telephone Number.* The telephone number to contact the **Stakeholder.**

Appendix 4:
Definitions of "Definition"

The following are definitions of the word "definition" taken from a list in Richard Robinson's book *Definition*. (See bibliography.)

Author	Definition
Plato [*Theaetetus,* 206C–7A, 208C]	1. Revealing one's thoughts by means of speech. 2. When someone asks you what a thing is, being able to answer him by means of the elements of the thing. 3. Being able to give some mark by which the thing asked about differs from all things.
Aristotle [*Topics* I, 5]	the account of the essence of the thing.
Cicero [*De Oratore,* I 42, 189]	a certain brief and circumscribed account of the properties of the thing we wish to define.
Milton [**Works**, (1851) IV 168]	that which refines the pure essence of things from the circumstance.
Spinoza [*Ethics,* I Prop. 8, n. 2]	the true definition of each thing involves nothing and expresses nothing but the nature of the thing defined.
Locke [*Essay*, III. iii. 10.]	making another understand by Words, what Idea the Term defined stands for.

Author	Definition
Kant [*Critique of Pure Reason*, A 727, tr. N. K. Smith	to present the complete, original concept of a thing within the limits of its concept.
J.S. Mill	a proposition declaratory of the meaning of a word; namely, either the meaning which it bears in common acceptation, or that which the speaker or writer, for the particular purposes of his discourse, intends to annex to it.
Whitehead and Russell [*Principia Mathematica*, 2nd ed., p. 11]	a declaration that a certain newly introduced symbol ... is to mean the same as a certain other combination of symbols of which the meaning is already known.
Wittgenstein [*Tractatus*, 3.343]	Definitions are rules for the translation of one language into another.
Carnap [*The Unity of Science*, tr. Max Black, p. 39]	a rule for mutual transformation of words in the same language.
Oxford English Dictionary	to state exactly what (a thing) is: to set forth or explain the essential nature of ... b: to set forth or explain what (a word or expression) means; to declare the signification of (a word). (Part of the article on 'define'.)

Appendix 5:
Examples of Definitions

Table A5.1: *Definition of Entity "Country" for Investment Bank X*

Summary Definition	An autonomously governed area of the world
Full Description	A country is a land area that has a government which is not subordinate to any other jurisdiction (super-national associations like the UN or European Union do not count).
Synonyms	"Territory," "National Jurisdiction," "Postal Country."
Homonyms	Occasionally we see in documentation that "country" is used to mean government of a country, or a specific agency of a government such as its taxation authority
Context	This definition is only known to apply to the North American Division. No contact has been made with the Asian, European, or Latin American Divisions. Within North America, we have sent the definition to all application support teams and have not received any questions, from which we infer that the definition applies to all applications.
Scope	Only countries that the company operates in or where its clients are domiciled are included in the Country table

Purpose	The company has the following reasons to use country: (a) As part of address – so country must always be a postal country. (b) To identify the ultimate jurisdiction for our operations in any location. (c) To identify the ultimate jurisdiction that applies to our clients.
Standard Used	We have adopted the ISO-3166 Alpha-2 code set for countries
Known Issues	(a) We have been asked by regulators to collect the countries of birth of all individuals. Some were born in countries that no longer exist, e.g. Soviet Union. We are currently trying to design a solution to this (b) "Hong Kong" is an entry in the central country table. Politically it is part of the People's Republic of China, but it seems to meet the needs of the organization. This situation will be reviewed in the Fiscal Year 2010. (c) The Marketing Division is exploring the use of countries, but their definition of a country as a sales territory may not match the one used here. The situation is under active discussion as of 1/1/2010. (d) See Accuracy for other issues.
Source	No external source was used for this definition. The definition was first formulated on 1/1/2008 by the Data Management Definition Working Group.
Stipulated Definition	Yes, (see source).

Legal Definition	No.
Accuracy	The extent of accuracy is not known. Five of the 10 databases in the North America Division have been profiled. The results are as follows: – Application A: 100 percent compatible with the central table of countries – Application B: 100 percent compatible with the central table of countries – Application C: The country table has regions and cities mixed in with countries – Application D: The country table has an entry for "XX." We do not know why – Application E: 100 percent compatible with the central table of countries No profiling has been done since 6/6/2009.

Table A5.2: *Definition of Column "Finance Charges" for Finance Company Y*

Underlined terms indicated hyperlinks.

Summary Definition	The interest and other relevant amounts payable by a <u>customer</u> for a loan at the end of every <u>payment cycle</u>.
Full Description	At the end of every <u>payment cycle</u> the <u>interest payable</u> is calculated on the <u>average loan balance</u> for each day from the start of the <u>payment cycle</u> using the <u>loan interest rate for the payment cycle.</u> To this are added any accrued <u>late charges</u> and any <u>NSF charges</u>. The sum of all these amounts is the Finance Charges.
Synonyms	"Monthly Finance Charge." (But the concept really applies only to a payment cycle, not a month.)
Homonyms	This term seems to be used in all kinds of places. It is often used in reports that aggregate Finance Charges. these reports are produced by the data warehouse
Business Rules	Finance Charges = <u>((Payment Cycle Average Loan Balance)</u> * <u>((Payment Cycle Loan Interest Rate)</u> / 360) * <u>(Number of Days in Payment Cycle))</u> + <u>(Accrued Late Charges)</u> + <u>(Accrued NSF Fees)</u>
Context	This definition is known only to be valid for the loan servicing application A. The definition has not been validated for the data warehouse, but it is doubtful that it applies there (see Homonyms).
Scope	Only personal loans have Finance Charges in the way that the term is defined here. The situation with institutional loans is not known

Purpose	To be able to bill each customer in accordance with the loan contract.
Standard Used	We have adopted the ISO-3166 Alpha-2 code set for countries
Known Issues	(a) The use of this term for concepts that are different from the one described here. There is a pending project that will review the use of all legal terms in computer applications and standardize them. It has been suggested that the term "Finance Charges" in the data warehouse be replaced by "Total Annual Finance Charges." However, little more is known about this situation.
Source	The Master Consumer Credit Agreement
Stipulated Definition	Yes. The definition has been created by the company
Legal Definition	Yes, based on the source.
Precision	To 2 decimal places, rounded to the nearest cent. Rounding errors are not material;
Accuracy	There are no known accuracy problems. Finance Changes are subject to periodic audit.

Bibliography

Baldwin, J. M. (ed.) *Dictionary of Philosophy and Psychology* (1905)

Collingwood, R. G. *The Idea of Nature* (1945)

Collingwood, R. G. *The Idea of History* (1946)

Collingwood, R. G. *An Essay on Philosophical Method* (1933)

Collingwood, R. G. *An Essay on Metaphysics* (1940)

Davidson, W. L. *The Logic of Definition* (1885)

Hammer M. & Champy J. *Reengineering the Corporation: A Manifesto for Business Revolution* (1993)

Harvey, C. *Campbell R. Harvey's Hypertextual Finance Glossary* http://www.duke.edu/~charvey/Classes/wpg/glossary.htm

Johnson, S. *A Dictionary of the English Language* (1755)

Joyce, G. H. *Principles of Logic* (1908)

Robinson, R. *Definition* (1950)

Shewhart, W. A. *Statistical method from the viewpoint of quality control* (1986 Edition)

Stanford Encyclopedia of Philosophy http://plato.stanford.edu/

Sullivan, S. *An Introduction To Traditional Logic: Classical Reasoning For Contemporary Minds* (2006)

Note: Unless specified otherwise, all URL's in this book were last accessed on February 15, 2010.

Index

f - figure
t = table

A

E

elliptical definitions, 111
emotive language, 125–126
Enterprise Data Management Council, 16
entities, glossary of, 219–221
entity instances, and producing definitions, 111–113
entity types
    and attributes, 130
    and concepts, 52
    defined, 67t
    existence of, 132–133
    metadata entity types, 197
    as metadata objects, 70–71
    and tables, 75–76
equivocal, 114
errors
    chance errors, 145
    and decay, 147–148
    systemic errors, 145
    timeliness, 147
    transcription errors, 148
essential characteristics, 59
essential definitions, 91–95
evaluation, 193
existence, 132–133
experts
    subject matter experts, 169–170, 176
    views on definitions, 15–19
explanations, in definitions, 126–127
extension, 152
external resources, 171

F

formal resources, 171
formal sign, 48
format, 197, 216

mental images, 42–45
metadata
    business-centric metadata, 202
    comments, 202–203
    versus data, 27
    data-centric metadata, 202
    defined, 195–196
    definition metadata, 198–199
    Dublin Core Metadata, 196–198, 215–218
    entity types, 197
    external organization metadata, 201
    history of definitions, 203
    model of, 199, 199*f*
    stakeholder metadata, 200–201
metadata objects
    attributes, 71–72
    business concepts, 69–70
    defines, 66
    entity types, 70–71
    relationships, 73, 74*f*, 75
    types of, 67–68*t*, 68–75
metadata versus data, 26–27
metrics, 149, 193–194
Mill, J. S., 64, 230
Milton, John, 229
modeling
    for definition metadata, 199, 199*f*
    of definitions, 84–86
    preliminary metamodel for definitions, 219*f*
    validation of, 87–88
monitoring, 192
Mukherjee, Arka, 16

N

NAICS, 28–29
natural language processing, 64
near indefinables, 105
negative definitions, 122–123
nominal definitions
    defined, 83

U

understandability analysis, 177
Universal Data Models LLC, 19
universal nature, 52

V

validation, 190–191
value, true, 145, 147
verb phrase, 73
verification, 190–191

W

Whitehead and Russell, 230
Wikipedia, 188–189
Wittgenstein, Ludwig, 88, 230
WorldNet example, 87*f*

Y

Yoakum-Stover, Suzanne, 19

Notes

Notes

Notes

Dr. Chisholm can be contacted via the companion web site for this book:
www.data-definition.com

CPSIA information can be obtained at www.ICGtesting.com
Printed in the USA
LVOW02*1605140814

399164LV00017B/740/P